SINGLE to SINGLE

ANTWAN STEELE

Brittany,

Thank you so much
for the support!

Much love,

Twan

TABLE OF CONTENTS

ISBN 978-0-9981512-0-5

For information regarding special discounts for bulk purchases, please contact info@antwansteele.com.

www.antwansteele.com

Cover design by Marcus Thomas

Printed in the United States of America

First Printing January 2017

DEDICATION

To Singles all over the country and world, I care about you. I understand this season of your lives can be challenging, but hang in there. This book is for you.

ACKNOWLEDGMENTS

First and foremost, I want to give all the glory and honor to my Lord and Savior, Jesus Christ. Your saving grace has transformed my life and I'm forever in debt to You. I'm so blessed to be Your son and I will continue to press on to live a life that is pleasing to Your Name. I love You more than anyone or anything. Thank You, Abba.

Mom and Dad, my favorite people on this side of heaven, I owe my life to you two. Your countless sacrifices over the years have led me to this point. I know at the end of the day, when all else is said and done, I can count on you both to be there for me. No one compares to you, not even a close second. I love you both with everything in me. I'm proud to call you my Parents. Thank you for establishing a legacy that will be passed down to my sisters and I.

Grandma Doris, your walk with God has been a major impact on my life. I'm so thankful for your ongoing intercession for me. You are the epitome of a prayer warrior. Thank you for also raising me. From the cooked meals to the long lectures, everything you've done for Jon and me is appreciated. Even those whoopings. My Lord, those whoopings. You are the backbone of this family and I love you for it.

Dominique and Taylor, I don't care how old you two are, the both of you will always be my baby sisters. Watching you both grow into becoming young adults has been amazing to witness and it inspires me to be better. You two mean so much to me and I'm so thankful to be your big brother. I love you.

Anthony Colbert, Demetri Crawley and Justin Boyd, you three are more than just my closest friends, you all are like brothers to me. Thank you for being by my side through the good and bad times. Your loyalty is a blessing to me. I'm beyond thankful for our brotherhood and look forward to strengthening our bond in the years to come.

Arrione Clark and Brittany Boyd, the ones who are responsible for the restructure of this book. Thank you for editing each line and seeing it through to completion. Thank you both for sticking it out with me even when I gave you push back. Thank you for the constant critique and honest feedback for the sake of producing quality work. You both were the most important people in getting this done and I owe it to you.

Pastor/Lady Vernon, my spiritual parents. Thank you for being great examples of how Christians should live. Thank you both for molding and shaping me into the man of God that I am today. Pastor, your sermons and wise counsel have been critical to my growth. Lady Vernon, thank you for always being warm and welcoming. I'm grateful to be under your leadership and thankful to be a member of The Word Church.

Dr. Bailey, I still remember the first time I met you and that day has set the tone for the type of relationship we have. You've been pulling the best out of me since then. You were more than just a boss to me, you were like a second mother. Thank you for helping me to mature as a professional. Thank you for helping me to realize my potential. Thank you for pouring into me wisdom that I can use for the rest of my life.

Cornelius Lindsey, although our friendship came later in life, I'm thankful that it has come. Since we've connected, you've been nothing but a blessing. I'll never take for granted the calls and texts just to check on me, and your willingness to support with nothing in return is humbling. You're an authentic and genuine person.

INTRODUCTION

WHY ANOTHER BOOK FOR SINGLES?

Firstly, I know there isn't anything new under the sun. Plenty of authors have written books for Singles. However, many of the authors writing for Singles are usually married. This doesn't mean married people cannot pen books for those of us who are unmarried, but what if there was a book written for Singles by someone who is Single? What if there was someone who could speak to Singles, while experiencing the same struggles. That would be me. As someone who understands the blessings and challenges of being Single, I can relate with those in the same boat as myself. My personal testimonies will allow you to connect with me and the lessons I've learned in this season will help you to grow.

Secondly, I've been burdened with the fact that hundreds of thousands of marriages end in divorce each year in the United States. These numbers make me wonder what these ex-spouses' lives were like before matrimony. Living in a society that doesn't honor and respect marriage the way God intended makes me concerned for Singles. Because the majority of us desire to be married, I have a strong desire to help Singles focus on preparing first and pursing second. Many times we have it backwards where we pursue first and prepare second. This is a preparation book with the hopes of guiding Singles in the right direction before making the second biggest decision of their lives.

Thirdly, I want you to have an intimate relationship with Christ. Accepting Him and following Him is the best decision you'll ever make in your life. Many of the books we read put so much emphasis on seeking love as if finding that someone is everyone's life mission. No, putting our faith in Christ and growing in our knowledge of Him everyday is our life's mission and it is extremely important for those of us who are Single to take heed to this wisdom. We as Singles must realize how crucial it is for us to start walking with God now. It will determine our path because He is the focal point, not a man, woman or marriage. We will be better for it in our future.

As you read what I've shared, I'm confident you'll gain valuable insight and learn from each chapter. Imagine you and I sitting across from each other at a coffee shop and I'm sharing with you my faults, lessons and victories in hopes that it will bless your journey.

So let us converse, Single to Single.

IDENTITY CHECK

I remember it like it was yesterday. "It's too packed in here," I thought to myself. There was no room to move. Everyone was shoulder to shoulder to the point where it was uncomfortable. On this particular Saturday night, I was at a popular bar, but the atmosphere felt more like a nightclub. I remained in the same spot for most of the night so that I wouldn't lose my seat; occasionally, I would signal to the bartender for another round. With a drink in my hand, I sat back and observed the crowd. Although I hadn't been out in awhile, I saw a lot of familiar faces from the last time that I was here. As time crept closer to the early morning hours, the crowd began to thin out. Finally, I started to move about and interact with those who lingered around after the last call.

"What's up man, what you been up to?", a guy I knew from around the way said to me. I replied, "Nothing much, just staying focused." He responded, "I remember when you were wild and reckless. But, now you've changed. That's what's up." I assumed that he said those things because I was no longer hanging out as much as I used to. In fact, I was just at Bible study on Wednesday, and in a few hours, I would be heading to church for Sunday service. I appreciated his acknowledgment. It made me feel like I was doing what I was supposed to do. I convinced myself that there was absolutely nothing wrong with being in bars or clubs and getting drunk with my friends, as long as I went to church, prayed, and occasionally read my Bible. As I left the bar late that night, I had no idea that God was preparing to radically transform my life within the next 24 hours.

The following morning I woke up to a call from Anthony, one of my closest friends who would help initiate the change in my life. As we started to converse, I instantly took notice to the difference in his voice. There was seriousness in his tone that I had never heard before. He shared with me his testimony about how he had given his life to Christ and strongly encouraged me to do the same. As he continued to talk about how God had set him free from his sinful past, I was shocked, yet proud to hear him share his sincerity for God without shame or timidity. I had never witnessed a young person that I could relate to express their love for God with such boldness. I was amazed.

After our call had ended, I stood in my kitchen deep in thought. "How could a man like Anthony, with all of the dirt that he and I have done together, give his life to Christ? I'm the one who's been taking him to church with me for the past three months. He hasn't even been in church that long," I thought to myself. I vividly recalled a Sunday in January when I headed over to Anthony's house to pick him up for church service. As he got in the car, I noticed that his eyes were hazy and slanted. I didn't want to assume, so I asked if he was high. His response was, "Yeah, it makes me think better when the pastor is preaching" (don't you laugh). I scolded him and told him to never do anything like that again, especially not around me. When we arrived at the sanctuary, the greeter leaned forward to hug us, but because he was under the influence, Anthony's first reaction was to put his hands up as if he was getting patted down. I was so embarrassed. After my initial shock had worn off, I found myself admiring the growth that my friend had just shown me by committing his life to Christ. As I reflected on this scenario and the conversation we'd just had, I knew that at times I had felt God tugging at my heart as well. I had consistently chosen to ignore His call. Right there, still standing in the kitchen, I began to ask myself, "What was preventing me from taking up my own cross and committing to following Jesus?"

> ## "I knew that at times I had felt God tugging at my heart as well."

I'd wrestled with the idea of submitting my life to Christ for years. Although I wanted to live for God because I knew that it was the right thing to do, a part of me wanted to continue to indulge in the things that I knew the Bible prohibited, like premarital sex and drunkenness. My life revolved around my desires and my selfishness, and I was accustomed to doing whatever I wanted to do without the fear of consequence. I knew that fornication was a sin, but I'd convinced myself that as long as I wasn't having intercourse with multiple women, sex outside of marriage wasn't "that bad." Or, that as long as I wasn't getting drunk or high every day, it was acceptable to do occasionally. The self-satisfying sins that I was committing seemed so innocent to me at that time, I didn't realize that I was blatantly rebelling against God. Some times, if ever did feel like I'd committed a sin, I thought that I could just say a quick sorry and move on with my life, with no real conviction or godly sorrow. Other times, when I felt any guilt about my wrongdoings, I thought I could just do something good to sooth my consciousness, but failed to ever truly repent. This morning, it was like a light-bulb had gone off and God had used Anthony to tell me that it was time to stop soothing and justifying and running from Him. I'd been telling myself that I was young and had all the time in the world, but God was telling me that the time was now. I'd feared the opinions of others, and I wanted to prevent being perceived as a hypocrite if I ever fell short, but God was telling me that His opinion is the only one that matters. I'd made every excuse as to why I didn't want to live for Him wholeheartedly. I wanted to be in control. I only wanted to obey God when it was convenient or beneficial for me, and I wanted to sin whenever my flesh desired. Obviously, I was lost.

I had come to the realization that I had one foot in the church and one foot in the world, and my inability to choose had left me straddling the fence. Although I had felt the inner pull at my soul, I was refusing to accept it due to the constant force of my flesh. But, even though I'd resisted, God had never given up on me. And now, He was giving me a divine ultimatum, Him or the world, and it was time to surrender to Him. It was as if God was using the transformation of someone close to me to finally get my attention, and it worked. I knew that if he could commit to God and allow Him to transform his life, then I could do the same.

After a brief moment of contemplation, I said to my Mother: "Mom, I'm changing my life." She responded nonchalantly, "That's good, baby." I said it again, "No, for real, Mom. I'm changing my life." I didn't realize that I wasn't changing a thing, but it was the power of God changing me. Nonetheless, I'd decided that I was truly going to live for God wholeheartedly. And, on April 10th, 2011 around 11 AM, God gifted me with salvation. It was as if an invisible weight was instantly lifted from my shoulders. I didn't care what anyone thought of my decision; I felt at peace knowing that the only approval that I needed to seek was His. For the first time in my life I had both of my feet firmly planted within the Kingdom, and by the grace of God, I finally began my walk with Christ.

WHAT DOES THIS STORY MEAN?

Before embarking on this journey with Christ, I never realized or heavily consider the many changes and sacrifices that this decision would entail. I've been traveling this path as a Single man for almost six years now, and everyday I am continuously learning. I've had both peak and pit moments that I'm honored to share with hopes that they will provide encouragement, guidance, and above all, the glorification of Christ. This book is not to be used as a blueprint for transformation or for the perfect recipe for a life in Christ, as there is no such thing. However, this is an honest recollection of my own experiences and the wisdom that I've gained over the years. I am confident that you and I will be able to connect with one another through my personal stories, biblical passages, and other useful information that will be shared throughout these pages. Furthermore, I am prayerful that after reading this book, you will be moved to accept or to grow closer to Christ, and make a lasting change towards living a life for Him in this season of your Singleness. There is no relationship status, whether single or married, that matters more than your relationship status with God. Once Christ came into my life, I realized that there was a significant difference between being Single in the world and being Single in the Kingdom. Which one are you? Do you know the difference?

Regardless of where you currently are in your life, God is ready to embrace you, forgive you, love you, and most importantly, He is ready to set you free. I know that it can be hard to confess sin and turn away from carnal living, especially when you're so used to it. When you are so accustomed to being in control of your life, it can be very difficult and even intimidating to learn how to trust God completely. But, once you surrender to Him, your life as a Single man or woman will never be the same. Believe me, I am a living testament to the saving grace of God.

> "Regardless of where you currently are in your life, God is ready to embrace you, forgive you, love you, and most importantly, he is ready to set you free."

WHO IS HE?

Jesus was God in the flesh, and He came to this earth for one specific reason, to die for our sins. The earth was sinful and the wages of sin is death. Because He loved us so much, God sent His Son as a sacrifice for our sins. Jesus was a perfect man. As He performed miracles and taught the truth, those who opposed Him sought to put a stop to the work that He was doing. Keep in mind, He never harmed anyone and lived a sinless life. Once Jesus was arrested after being betrayed, He was brought in front of the Jewish leaders to be interrogated for His claims of being the Son of God. Because Jesus remained silent to their questions, the soldiers repeatedly struck Him in the face, taunted, and even spat on Him.

The next morning Jesus was brought to the Roman Governor who was pressured by the Jews and the crowd to execute Him, even though there was no crime committed. The same crowd that had praised Jesus a few days prior was now lobbying for His crucifixion. At the request of the people, Barabbas, a notorious murderer, was released from prison in exchange for Jesus to be tormented and murdered. Jesus was stripped of His clothing and had His hands tied to a post. The Roman guard took out a heavy whip with thongs and sharp objects at the tips and struck Jesus repeatedly. His skin began to rip to the point where His bones were visible, and an unrecognizable Jesus collapsed in a pool of His own blood.

After the brutal torture, the Roman guards continued to taunt Jesus by putting a robe around Him, and mocking His claim of being King. They made a crown of thorns and forcefully placed it on His head, which pierced deep into His scalp. Soon, they began beating Him again. When the time came for Jesus to be crucified, He was forced to carry His own cross along the road called Via Dolorosa, which some scholar's claim was the length of six to seven football fields. Due to an abundant loss of blood and a severely beaten body, Jesus was physically incapable of carrying His cross. With help, He made it to Calvary, the place He would be crucified.

As Jesus was positioned on the wooden cross, two long iron stakes were put through His wrists until they were visible on the other side of the cross. Jesus' feet were placed together in an extended position and another iron stake was forced through the arch of His feet. As Jesus hung from this cross He endured excruciating pain. Each time that He pushed Himself up to breathe, the stakes tore through the flesh of His feet. His arms suffered from intense cramping and fatigue. Eventually, He began to suffocate. The many lacerations on His back rubbed against the rough timber as He moved up and down the cross trying to find comfort. The fullness of God's wrath poured out onto Jesus, as He bore the sins of the entire world. At this moment, God turned His back on His only begotten Son and Jesus experienced separation from His Heavenly Father. He began to cry out. When Jesus finally says, "it is finished," He commits His Spirit to Glory. This act of selflessness and torment is what

He experienced for you. Jesus died so that you could live.

> ## "Jesus died so that you could live."

Jesus experienced abandonment, betrayal, hate, injustice, pain, rejection, and more until His death. But, why would He allow Himself to be humiliated in such a way? Romans 5:8 tells us, "But God demonstrates his own love for us in this: While we were still sinners, Christ died for us." Although we may be aware of Jesus' death, sometimes we can forget what His sacrifice truly means. His willingness to suffer and die for us, regardless of how damaged we may be, speaks to the type of love that we can only receive from Him.

I know you are probably wondering what this has to do with your identity? Believe me, it has everything to do with who you are. Before you can know your real value, you must first understand that Christ paid His life for you. That act alone is the ultimate example of how much He loves you and how much you are worth to Him. Take His sacrifice personal. His unconditional, undying and unfailing love is for you. You are accepted, empowered, forgiven, loved and purposed by Christ. Before I discuss with you the importance of knowing who you are, you must first know Whose you are. Yes, this knowledge is relevant to everyone, but it is essential for Single men and women.

The reason why this relates to Singleness is because society loves to brand those of us who are not married. It seems as if the world likes to categorize Singles as a group of people who are desperate for love, immature because we lack the responsibility of a marriage, and possibly even unlovable if no one has "chosen" you by a certain age. We experience an overwhelming amount of societal pressure—from our parents, family and friends, churches, etc.—for being unmarried, and its time that we focus less on how we are labeled and more on defining our worth. When we as Singles can welcome all that we are in Christ, regardless of what society tells us, we can rest in the value given to us by our Heavenly Father.

Foundation is crucial for anything worth building. It's the anchor of all existence and the root of all growth. Anything that is created to produce, but lacks a solid structure will eventually collapse. With that said, Christ is the foundation for every Single. Without Him, we have no origin. I've observed many Singles over the years, including myself, who have battled with identity issues. Most of the time, we're blind to the fact that we struggle with our identity in the first place. Thankfully, all of our answers can be found in God who is the Exemplifier of humanity. I want you to see yourself the way The Lord sees you.

When you realize who you are in Christ, it will revolutionize your perspective of self and appreciation for Him.

WHO ARE YOU?

There is only one person in all of the humanity who was born married, and that was Eve. She was never a girlfriend or a fiancée; she was created as a wife. Adam and every other human being in the history of humankind were born unmarried. There is significance in this. Just as we are created as human beings, we are created as Single people. So, if we start our lives with Singleness, shouldn't we discover our identity in this specific season? Shouldn't we first know who we are and have a desire to live a life pleasing to God before we enter into covenant marriage with a spouse if that is even in His will for us?

> "Just as we are created as human beings, we are created as Single people."

Should we base our worth off of what others think of us? Of course not! If we based our value solely on the opinions of others that would mean that we are aiming to please people and not Christ. Should our significance be determined by our past mistakes? Absolutely not! We all have made mistakes, and those misfortunes can be used as lessons to help us grow. Should we define ourselves by what we do for a living and by the accomplishments that we achieve? Not at all! Our job titles and accomplishments seem like a great way to determine our identity. However, the problem with this approach is that we will have to retain these titles and sustain that lifestyle of accomplishments to continually validate our worth. That cannot be what identity is all about. How we identify ourselves is the type of attitude and philosophy that we will take when approaching our lives. So again, who are we?

People are infatuated with the greatness of mountains, serenity of oceans, brilliance of stars and beauty of nature as if it was God's greatest work. We travel thousands of miles across the world to experience the wonders of the earth, but we forget that we are God's greatest creation. Yes, you are God's greatest creation. At our very core, we are formed in the image of God, and that includes both male and female. No, God's character was not portrayed in just one gender. Man and woman were made equal, yet for different roles. We weren't mistakes when we were created, and we definitely aren't mistakes now. Being created in the image of God means we are made to resemble Him. We are to bear His likeness. We represent our God by being creative, emotional, intellectual, moral, personal, relational and spiritual.

Before accepting Christ as my personal Savior, I was lost in the worldly way of living. Although I wasn't truly following Christ at the time, I was still someone made in the image of God. But, bearing the likeness of God didn't mean that I was saved. Only when Christ occupied my heart did I become a Believer, and from that point on, I had a new identity in Christ. Here is a brief list of who the Bible says that I am and you are, as a Believer:

- **YOU ARE** redeemed and forgiven
- **YOU ARE** a child of God
- **YOU ARE** a whole new person
- **YOU ARE** a friend of Jesus
- **YOU ARE** free from sin
- **YOU ARE** a citizen of Heaven
- **YOU ARE** the righteousness of God
- **YOU ARE** a partaker of His promise
- **YOU ARE** complete in Christ
- **YOU ARE** the light of the world
- **YOU ARE** spiritually alive
- **YOU ARE** deeply loved
- **YOU ARE** the temple of God's Spirit

I could go on and on about all of the great things that the Bible has to say about you through Christ, but what makes it even more amazing is that you don't have to do anything to earn these things. Your identity isn't achieved; it's received. All you have to do is accept it. Because God made you, He has the power to define you and approve you. It is all Him. This undeserved uniqueness given to us by God should be liberating. Only from this spiritual understanding can we learn how to develop into the men and women we are called to be. The world defines you by your past, but The Lord gives you hope for a future. The world accepts you only when it's beneficial, but The Lord accepts you just the way you are. The world will waiver in its commitment to you, but The Lord is the same as yesterday, today and forever. Put your trust in the God of all creation for He is the God who loves you with a matchless love.

> "The world defines you by your past, but The Lord gives you hope for a future. The world accepts you only when it's beneficial, but The Lord accepts you just the way you are. The world will waiver in its commitment to you, but The Lord is the same as yesterday, today and forever."

WHY ARE YOU HERE?

Life doesn't stop at salvation. Otherwise, you would have gone to Heaven the moment that you accepted Christ. Once you know who He is and what He has done for you, it leads you to know who you are and why you were created. John Piper explained it concisely by saying, "The true significance of life is that God made human beings in His own image with precious value and that value, that significance insists in knowing God, loving God and showing God." We want to know Christ so that we can become more like Him. We want to love Christ so we can develop an intimate relationship with Him. We want to show Christ so we can inspire others to do the same for Him. These acts are our meaningful existence.

Firstly, knowing God starts with accepting Jesus Christ as Savior and Lord. We acknowledge Him as our Savior because He died for our sins, which we repent for and put our trust in Him. Then, we surrender our will to His by making Him Lord over every area of our lives. John 17:3 says, "And this is eternal life, that they know you the only true God and Jesus Christ whom you have sent." From there we can grow closer to Him through prayer and the studying of Scripture so that we reflect Him in our daily living. We must be intentional and persistent about getting to know Him.

Secondly, once we know God, we can love God. John 14:15 says, "If you love Me, you will keep My commandments." For starters, loving Christ is all about obeying Him. There's no way around it. You cannot, and I repeat, you cannot claim to love Christ if you are unwilling to follow what He commands. This doesn't mean that you won't fall short, but because you love Him, you will have a heart to do what is pleasing in His sight. As we keep His commands, love will flow to Him and to others, and that embodies the love of God.

Thirdly, as Christ reveals knowledge of Himself and our relationship with Him is deepened, we'll want to share Him with the world. Luke 8:16 says, "No one lights a lamp and hides it in a clay jar or puts it under a bed. Instead, they put it on a stand, so that those who come in can see the light." When God has revealed to us His power and splendor, we will want to showcase Him. We will desire to spread His Word to others so that they can also know and love Him, and in return, they will introduce Him to others.

It's imperative for Singles to understand the reason why we were created. Knowing God, loving God, and showing God takes precedence over everything in your life. Life is, has always been, and will always be about God. It also sets the tone for every chapter to follow in this book. Allow this Truth to become a reality in your Season of Singleness.

MY PAST HASN'T PASSED

"Hey Twan,

I really don't know how to start this, but I need your help. You posted something yesterday, and the caption really motivated me. As you know, my past is really dark, from family issues to drugs to promiscuity. I feel like something is holding me back from fully giving my life to Christ. Twan, honestly, you and several other men used to degrade me sexually, and I allowed it, because "I wanted you to like me." However, I take full responsibility for my actions, but I can't escape it. I'm so proud of you, but tell me how you put your past behind you? It's really haunting me deep down. I really have so much to say but can't find the words. Please help."

I received this email from a woman of my past. I could have shared this later on in the fifth chapter of this book to prove my point about the lasting effects of premarital sex, but I believe this situation is more relevant here. Just as this woman was dealing with the issues of her past, which I was involved in, many Singles are also struggling with pain from their pasts. One thing that the Bible guarantees us is that we will experience hardships. We live in an imperfect world, and no one is exempt from facing sorrow and troubles in this life. The difficulties that we face aren't destined to defeat us, even though they're designed to. The internal damages we've suffered as a result of our pasts can lead to brokenness that can lead to the building of invisible walls around our hearts, guarding us against being further wounded. Our hearts may eventually become cold and hardened by the pain, and it hinders us from healing and living an emotionally free life. I'm speaking from first-hand experience.

> ## "The difficulties that we face aren't destined to defeat us, even though they're designed to."

A wise man once said, "If I can be a young man, you can be an old boy." I've interpreted this statement to mean that many Single adults may have matured physically and financially, but not mentally and emotionally. There's a large group of Single men and women who are so emotionally damaged from their past, that they've never healed from what they've endured. I'll be the first to admit that it took me a while to understand that I was still struggling with issues from my past even after I was saved. Initially, I thought that once I submitted my life to Christ that everything that I had previously gone through didn't matter anymore. While that is partially true, there is still work that needs to be done so that deliverance can take place.

One reason why we struggle with our identity is because we've been hurt in our past. But regardless of who or what hurt you, and how and why it happened, it's time to face it and let it go. It's time that you forgive and heal. Letting go of the past and getting whole is crucial, especially in your season of Singleness. Let's discuss.

DEEPLY WOUNDED

When someone suffers from a physical wound, there are healing stages that take place within the body to repair the injured area. Generally speaking, some wounds heal quicker than others depending on the severity of the damage done. Plus, your attention and treatment to the wound will also play a significant role in the recovery period. Follow me? Once the wound occurs, the blood begins to clot, creating a scab. After the scab has formed, the immune system begins to cleanse the area to remove any bacterial infections. In a few days, the body will start to repair the damaged tissue, providing a new layer of skin. Eventually, the only evidence left of the old wound will be a scar, and even that has the potential to fade away over time. Nonetheless, the pain is gone, and the wound has healed. Because this process is visible to the human eye and we can see it taking place, the healing of external wounds is much easier to gauge than internal wounds.

In your season of Singleness, it's typical to focus on becoming physically healthy, but there is much less emphasis on becoming emotionally healthy. The wounds that we endure from our experiences in life can have lasting detrimental effects, and if not cared for properly, they may never heal. Abandonment, betrayal, loss, neglect, and rejection are five of the most common causes of emotional wounds. Abandonment is when someone leaves or gives up on you. Betrayal is when someone has broken a bond or trust. Loss is when someone or something is taken from you. Neglect is when someone fails to care for you. Rejection is when you are denied something that you want or need. Experiencing one or more of these common causes of emotional wounds can produce additional unhealthy feelings such as anger, bitterness, depression, fear, guilt, pride, or shame.

John Bloom, Editor at Desiring God, said, "God designed your emotions to be gauges, not guides. They're meant to report to you, not dictate you." Our emotions should be used as an alert system to make us aware of the breach in our hearts. Every day we have the choice of dealing with our past the right way or the wrong way. The right decision will lead to the freedom of forgiveness, whereas the wrong decision will burden us with the weight of unforgiveness. Have you forgiven those who have abandoned, betrayed, neglected, rejected, or hurt you? Do you have an unforgiving heart? Keep reading.

> "Our emotions should be used as an alert system to make us aware of the breach in our hearts."

AN UNFORGIVING HEART

Emotional wounds are further infected by unforgiveness. Choosing not to forgive someone is like persistently picking at the scab of a wound; it slows the healing process. The issue with unforgiveness is that it's rooted in distrust of God's righteousness. A Single's refusal to forgive or struggle with forgiveness shows a lack of faith in God to bring forth justice. When someone has wronged you, you expect for them to pay for their sin, and may sometimes even believe it's your responsibility to see that this punishment takes place. Other times, we say we trust God to handle it, but when He doesn't punish those who have hurt us as quickly or harshly as we think they should be, we grudgingly hold on to what they did to us. We are unable to move on until they "get what they deserve". However, if we truly trust God, we must also trust that in His time, He will bring forth justice. It is our only responsibility to lay the problem at His feet and to acknowledge and repent for our wrongdoings, instead of focusing on the punishment of others. Don't walk in the victimization of your innocence, but soar in the freedom of your own deliverance.

> ## "Don't walk in the victimization of your innocence, but soar in the freedom of your own deliverance."

Emotional wounds can heal once forgiveness takes place. Not only do we forgive for our sake, but also we forgive because God forgave us. Christ's crucifixion should be embedded into our hearts so that whenever we're tempted not to forgive or delay in our forgiveness, the Holy Spirit will convict us. If we have our minds fixed on the brutal suffering that Christ endured on the cross for us, how can we not forgive? Forgiveness precedes healing.

Look back over your life. What are you holding on to? When did your heart turn cold? How is it that you were once the sweetest girl or the nicest guy, but no longer want to be identified as such? Is it a failed relationship? Is it a parent who was never in your life or maybe they were physically present but emotionally absent? Is it the person who picked on you when you were a child? Is it church hurt? Is it a friend who betrayed you? Is it the death of a family member? Is it molestation or rape? Is it a tragic event that occurred? Even more, is it something you haven't for-

MY PAST HASN'T PASSED

given yourself for? Let us not forget that forgiveness is not a feeling; it's a choice. Your past does not have to dictate your future. Choose forgiveness and allow God to heal you.

HEALING OUR WOUNDS

Everyone will experience some form of pain and sorrow in their lifetime. No one is wound-proof, but we can be wound-free if we take the proper steps to heal. Unfortunately, there are no shortcuts for this process. However, I will discuss five essential steps that can lead you towards a path of forgiveness and healing.

Acknowledge

God won't heal what you keep concealed. Sweeping your emotions under the rug eliminates your chances of being liberated from all of your past hurt. Many Singles aren't mindful of how to deal with the emotional wounds of their lives because they have failed to acknowledge that they exist. We can't just go through life with unchecked emotions. We have to face issues as they arise, and also dig deep into our hearts to address the issues from our pasts that continue to haunt us. Healing begins with a humble confession to God about the troubles of your heart. God is pleased when we share with Him our feelings. Think about the story of Job who suffered great loss of his family and possessions. He prayed to God with an unfiltered transparency, and didn't shy away from what he was going through. Transparency is defined as allowing light to pass through so that objects behind can be distinctly seen. We need the light of Christ to shine through the barriers and layers of our hearts so that emotional wounds can be revealed to us so that we can address them.

As a previous employee of the Cancer Outreach Department at Cleveland Clinic, I had the opportunity of working with many different people in the community. In regards to physical health, my department was adamant about early detection and preventative care. We encouraged our patients to stay up to date on their screenings because it is much easier to treat cancer if it's caught in earlier stages than if it's detected in the later stages. What made my job difficult is that some patients would prolong scheduling an appointment, even if they were experiencing painful symptoms, because they feared the worst. I remember urging an older patient to see his primary care doctor as soon as possible so that they could address his failing health. His response, "I'll just die with this."

The point that I'm making is that there is a Great Physician who's readily available to heal what's going on inside of us, but we have to first go to Him with the problem. Furthermore, we need a trusted friend who we can be completely open and honest with. Sharing our deepest and darkest struggles with another person allows everything we're dealing with to come to the surface of our hearts instead of remaining hidden within it.

Access

After acknowledging the problem, you can now pinpoint the emotional wound. Who hurt you? What happened? When did it happen? Where did it happen? Reliving these memories might make you feel uncomfortable, but the purpose is for you to face the pain so that you can be free from it. Many Singles fail to reach this stage of healing because the thought of getting to the root cause of their wounds seems too painful and difficult, and they believe that the pain will eventually disappear over time. There is a common misconception that we can just get over our emotional wounds. But, the truth is, without doing the necessary work, we never get over the pain; instead, we just become really good at concealing it. Why live your life harboring deep-rooted pain when you can be delivered from it?

Imagine having a garden. You have an enormous field of fertile land that has the potential of reaping a plentiful harvest, but there are all of these pesky weeds that keep sprouting up. Whenever you see a weed, you cut it down. But, ten more seem to pop up in its place, and it hinders the growth of your garden. Finally, it dawns on you: Instead of cutting the weeds at the surface level, you need to access their core and uproot them from the land so they won't grow again.

This is exactly what we have to do to our pain. Our hearts have the potential of giving and receiving an abundance of love, but we have to access the weeds that linger in our souls and uproot them so that we can blossom the way Christ intended us to. Many Singles don't want to do the dirty work of getting on their knees so that they can be unchained from the roots of their pain. This is critical to bring forth healing and restoration to our souls.

Accept

"God grant me the serenity to accept the things I cannot change, the courage to change the things I can, and the wisdom to know the difference." We all know this as the Serenity Prayer, but I like to think of it as the Acceptance Prayer. These powerful words are vital to the healing process because they remind us not to dwell on the things that are out of our control and to redirect our focus to the areas where we can improve. Let me be clear: You are not to blame for every horrible thing that has happened to you in your life. Certain circumstances will be completely out of your hands. But, even in those moments when you can't change the outcome, make the conscious decision to learn from your pain and be a better person because of it.

In addition to accepting the uncontrollable, the most critical part of this stage of healing is accepting that God loves you with an everlasting, incomparable, never-failing, undying love. Open your heart up to Him and receive this cure for your soul. Knowing that God is a loving God isn't enough for us if we don't believe it for ourselves. Accept that God accepts you. Let this truth marinate in your heart and eventually the forgiveness of self and the forgiveness of others won't seem like such a difficult decision.

> ## "It's impossible to embrace the fullness of Christ while clinging to the emptiness of your hurt."

I know that this phase of healing can be hard. You may have been through some heartbreaking, mind-altering, and soul-crushing circumstances, and are still struggling to accept what has happened to you. We're only human, so it's completely natural to feel the way that you feel. However, you must have faith that God will deliver and heal you. What will you accept, God's love or your pain? One has to go. It's impossible to embrace the fullness of Christ while clinging to the emptiness of your hurt.

Affirm

Encouragement is refreshing to the soul. It's like ice-cold water on a scorching hot summer day. Being affirmed is essential in keeping you on the right path towards healing, particularly when you aren't feeling at your best. This encouragement and support should come from three sources: yourself through faith; a community of Believers through fellowship; and most importantly, from God through His Word.

I can recall many instances when I didn't have anyone around. The enemy would continually attack my mind with thoughts of my past mistakes. Instead of believing those lies or dwelling in that negativity, I chose to speak life over myself. I had to call myself blessed. I had to remind myself that I'm doing well. I had to meditate on Scriptures like Philippians 4:8, and I still do. It says, "Finally, brothers and sisters, whatever is true, whatever is noble, whatever is right, whatever is pure, whatever is lovely, whatever is admirable--if anything is excellent or praiseworthy--think about such things." There will be days when it's just you. God may be silent (even though He's still there), and family and friends may be absent. Get in the habit of encouraging yourself.

In most cases, when we're hurt we tend to cut people off or shut down altogether. Obviously, this does more harm than it does good. We can become emotionally starved if we don't have the encouragement from our relationships to nourish our souls. We need meaningful fellowship from those we trust. Surround yourself with people who can uplift you when you feel that your past is trying to pull you down. 1 Thessalonians 5:11 says, "Therefore encourage one another and build one another up, just as you are doing."

> ## "We can become emotionally starved if we don't have the encouragement from our relationships to nourish our souls."

Above all, the Bible should be our primary source for an emotional remedy. Psalm 119:28 says, "My soul is weary with sorrow; strengthen me according to your word." When we're in dire need of some internal inspiration, we must lean on His Word. Reading Scriptures isn't just about gaining biblical knowledge; it's also about understanding the God of the Bible. Every story in these 66 books is a testimony about the works of Jesus Christ. As we meditate on His Word, we can be sure that it will speak to our current condition and give us hope to press on. Not only is the Word a mirror to our souls, but it's also a lamp to our feet and the light to our path. As we study the Scriptures, it will uncover the vulnerability in our hearts and will help guide us along the way to deliverance. When our emotions or reactions are out of sync, we can simply align them with what God commands and watch how the obedience brings forth a healing that we could have never imagined.

Act

It's time to take action. Some Singles will be connected to your purpose through your pain. 1 Corinthians 1:4 says, "He comforts us in all our troubles so that we can comfort others. When they are troubled, we will be able to give them the same comfort God has given us." Please know that God never allows our struggles to be in vain. Where you're the most deeply wounded is where God may be preparing to use you. An encouraging sign of freedom from emotional bondage is when you're able to boldly share your story in hopes that it will liberate others. Who is more qualified to help a Single who is going through heartbreak than someone who's been healed of heartbreak? Who can better help a Single who is dealing with parent issues than someone who's been delivered from parent issues? Who can provide more understanding to a Single who's been molested than someone who's been healed of molestation?

As you go through the process of healing, prepare yourself to be used as a vessel to help others heal as well. Look for Single brothers and sisters to serve. You must take the initiative in helping others because what you've survived is a testimony that can assist someone else in their breakthrough. Even more, your survival is an absolute blessing and serves as proof that God can turn our mess into ministries. Use what you've been through to help others get through, and they'll do the same for someone else. That's what Romans 8:28 means when it says, "And we know that in all things God works for the good of those who love him, who have been called according to his purpose."

Emotional healing isn't something that happens overnight, it occurs over time. Your heart doesn't scream out, 'I'm healed!' Instead, your progress becomes visible in your everyday life when you face conflicts. Your reactions speak to the healing in your heart. When you've reached a point in your life where what you've gone through doesn't impact you the same way that it once did, that is a clear indication that you are healing. I am healing ♡

WEIGHT OF THE WAIT

A couple from my church was having a gathering at their home and asked me if I'd like to join them. I happily accepted their invitation, and I was glad to hear that other Singles were expected to attend (hey, no one wants to be the only one without a plus one at a party). When I arrived, I felt somewhat anxious when I realized that the majority of those who had actually shown up were married couples. As a Single man in my late twenties, I've had some interesting conversations and debates with spouses about my Singleness, and they always seem to end with them trying to perform a holy hook up. Nonetheless, I was amongst friends, so everything was cool.

The night was going smoothly. The conversation was great, the food was delicious, and the vibes were pleasant. Overall, I was in good company and really enjoying myself. But, then the question that every Single hates to answer was asked, "So Twan, when are you getting married?" With every ear bent towards my response, I casually stated, "Whenever God sees fit." Then the floodgate of questions came pouring in. "Do you have a potential? What is your type? Do you even want to be married? What are you waiting for?" I felt like I was in the middle of an interrogation room. Although they meant well, it was frustrating being asked the same questions over and over again.

Frankly, what I wanted to tell them was that I never imagined that I'd be a Single man going into my 30s. I actually don't think any Single does unless they've never desired to be married. For as long as I can remember, I've always wanted to be married and have a family, and I still do. As a Single, it can be tough when this desire has yet to be fulfilled, and it's even more challenging when I'm constantly being pressured (like they were currently doing to me). But instead, I just smiled and pretended as if I didn't feel like the elephant in the room.

As the night came to a close, most people left with their spouses, while I left all alone and feeling worst than when I first arrived. The pressure from everyone weighed heavily on me. Thoughts of anxiousness, frustration, insignificance, and loneliness clouded my mind the entire ride home, and I began to believe that I needed to be married.

This is an example of the weight of the wait. As you can see from my experience, this period of waiting wouldn't be as heavy if outside influences weren't a factor. The pressures that Singles deal with can impact our decisions to marry prematurely. Conversely, societal problems in modern times have a significant responsibility in the prolonging of marriage for Singles as well. In this chapter, we'll discuss these ongoing struggles in the season of waiting.

PRESSURED FROM ALL SIDES

All throughout life, we've been conditioned for the next big thing, and it starts in our teenage years. We're told to graduate from high school with good grades, earn a degree or two from college, and then climb the corporate ladder within the right corporation. Ultimately, this leads to the most important goal, which is to get married and start a family. Yes, I said goal because many times marriage is treated as if it's the number one objective of our lives. Actually, it's treated more like the beginning of the end because the next best thing that you have to look forward to after marriage is your retirement (with your spouse, of course).

From generation to generation, society has developed this milestone mentality that every Single must attain. Don't get me wrong; marriage is a beautiful thing to desire. But in reality, millions of Singles aren't hitting the marriage milestone, and this is where it becomes challenging. When you're in your late teens or even your early 20s, marriage isn't much of a big deal. But, as you edge closer to 30, it's as if everyone's marriage antennas go up. Singles become criticized by society for not having a spouse. Because our culture is so couple-oriented and relationship-driven, we're forced to believe that Singles of a certain age must be doing something wrong if they are unmarried.

> "Because our culture is so couple-oriented and relationship-driven, we're forced to believe that Singles of a certain age must be doing something wrong if they are unmarried. "

It seems as if the moment that you start to embrace and feel comfortable in your Singleness, society finds a way to remind you that you are spouseless. If you're spending time with family, there's pressure. If you're hanging out with friends, there's pressure. If you're at work, there's pressure. If you're serving in church, there's pressure. The constant nagging or endless reminders that we need to be with someone can be burdensome. Can you relate? Let's talk about the many pressures that we may face as Singles.

Family Pressure

At every family function, I can guarantee one of my relatives will ask me about my plans for marriage. Believe me, it never fails. Typically, our families are the closest to us, and they tend to have the greatest impact on the life decisions that we make. The members of our family want nothing more than to see us with someone who makes us happy because our happiness is important to them. But, when your aunts and uncles keep pressing you about why it didn't work out with the last person you brought to the cookout, and your parents keep asking you when you are going to give them grandchildren, it can easily begin to feel like your Singleness is letting them down. You may even feel like you're coming up short or empty-handed every time that you show up to a family gathering without a potential spouse.

If you're like me, you look forward to the day when you can enjoy your wedding with your family. You can't wait to be walked down the aisle by your father; perform a Youtube-worthy dance with your mother; or, shed tears after a heartfelt speech from your siblings. As much as you want to celebrate this joyous moment with your loved ones, you can rest assured they desire the same thing. Again, they only want to see you happy. That's the reason why they bombard us with questions about our relationships, or lack thereof. I know that the constant probing about marriage can sometimes get annoying but try to remember that their questions come from a place of love. But I know, nonetheless, it's still pressure. The weight of the wait.

Married Friends' Pressure

"Just because your friends are doing it doesn't mean you have to do it. If all of your friends jumped off a bridge would you do it, too?" My Mother used to say this to me all of the time when I was younger. Today, if I replaced the word bridge with broom, and chose to jump because all of my friends did, my Mother might actually be happy (just kidding, Mom). As a Single with married friends, you may feel like the oddball or even left out of the group. In my case, all three of my closest friends tied the knot within a two-year period of each other. So, you can probably imagine how I felt. They had each jumped off the bridge of Singleness, and there I was, still sitting there as I heard the echoes of their voices saying, "jump, jump, jump!"

While my friends rarely questioned me about my love life, the pressures I felt from them to jump the gun stemmed from feeling like an outsider within my own inner circle. The people that I hung with the most had added spouses to their lives, and I instantly became the third, fifth, and eventually, the seventh wheel. Yikes! This wasn't by any means their fault, but initially, it was tough to deal with. Imagine being at dinner with your married friends, and they start having conversations about "married folks" issues, but because you're Single and can't quite relate, you just sit there awkwardly and hope that they'll soon switch the topic. Imagine having to endure their moments of overt affection right in front of your face. Imagine taking a group picture and being the only one who isn't coupled up. Talk about pressure. These are the type of struggles that us Singles have to deal with from our marital crew. The weight of the wait.

Workplace Pressure

Being in the work environment is slightly different because there is a level of professionalism that is expected, but even that doesn't deter colleagues from nitpicking at your love life. Comments like "you better find someone soon because you're not getting any younger" was a favorite amongst my team. Although I felt the least amount of marital pressure in the workplace, there were also moments that I felt less respected because of my Singleness. In previous positions, I observed that management offered more leniency to those who were married, and simply because I was Single I was expected to work later or come in on the weekends. Many colleagues assumed that I wasn't serious about my life or career because I was unmarried, as if a Single can't be ambitious or want to work hard just for themselves. I once had a conversation with a woman in upper management, and she said, "Those who are married are more respected than those who are unmarried. Marriage speaks to a sense of responsibility and those who have spouses are more likely to handle leadership roles much better." How disappointing is it that your ability to lead may be determined by whether or not you have a ring on the fourth finger of your left hand? The weight of the wait.

Church Pressure

This may or may not be surprising, but I've experienced an immense amount of pressure to be married from other Christians, especially within my church. Because the community of Believers has such a high regard for marriage, this deep reverence permeates the atmosphere of the church. From the pulpit to the parking lot, there have been numerous occasions when I've felt like my Singleness was treated more like an issue that needed to be resolved rather than supported. Sometimes it seems like the general message for Singles in the church is about finding a spouse instead of finding completion in Christ. Singles can feel like second-class Christians in their own churches

> "Sometimes it seems like the general message for Singles in the church is about finding a spouse instead of finding completion in Christ."

One Sunday morning after service, I wanted to share an issue that had been weighing heavily on my heart with one of the leaders at my church. As I approached him and began to express my thoughts, he interrupted me by saying, "What do you think about this girl behind you? Wait, don't look yet. Okay, now look." As I turned around to see who he was talking about, I turned back to him and said, "No." I then tried to finish sharing my thoughts when he interrupted me again, saying, "You sure you're not interested?" By that time I was frustrated. I was seeking spiritual counsel, but he was more focused on trying to find me a wife. Now, this isn't meant to bash the church. I know that it comes from a place of good intent and love. But, it can be exhausting for Singles when the constant marital pressures we feel from the outside world are also felt when we enter into our place of worship. The weight of the wait.

When society puts pressure on Singles to be married, it tends to make us feel restless when it doesn't happen. We begin to feel like we're missing out on something, and this makes it difficult for us to wait on God. Along with all of the external pressures that we face, Singles can also place added pressure on themselves. Single women may worry about their biological clocks, and Single men may fear that they won't have children who will carry on their legacy.

These issues are serious. In a society that glorifies marriage and demeans Singleness, how can it not be difficult for us? These pressures only magnify the problem by exposing our heart and influencing us to expedite the process. Listen, instead of rushing into a marriage for social acceptance, wait until you receive the peace of God's approval.

THE WEIGHT OF THE TIMES

As if the pressures that come from society, family, friends, workplace and church aren't enough, Singles are also facing generational issues that impact the age at which they get married. In the 1950's, people were marrying in their early 20's. In this day and age, people are getting married in their late 20's. So, why the dramatic change? The causes are different for every Single. Some of the problems that keep us in our season of Singleness are out of our control while others are directly connected to the decisions that we make. Here's variety of issues that are prolonging marriage for Singles.

Economic Focus

In today's time, many Singles have a better understanding of the importance of financial security and are choosing to delay marriage until they have established themselves. More Single men and Single women are seeking careers and degrees before a family. These accomplishments give them a greater sense of confidence in their financial stability. This can be a wise thing to do considering that financial issues are a leading cause of divorce. As the rich continues to get richer and the poor continues to get poorer, the number of those getting married may continue to decrease, and this extends the waiting season.

Clashing Genders

Do girls really run the world? Or, is it true that this is a man's world? People have been trying to figure this out since the beginning of time. This distracting battle of who's more significant is a tool that the enemy uses to perpetuate division; sadly, these clashing perspectives are also leading to dysfunction between Single men and women. I once read an article that asked if men are superior to women. To ask the question was a problem in itself, but it was the responses that made it even more discouraging. As each gender took constant shots at each other, I was reminded of where Singles stand in this ongoing battle of the sexes. As this continues to be the pulse of our society, it makes it harder for marriages to manifest. Males want to remain bachelors because they fear being controlled by a woman. Females would rather be seen as independent women because they don't want to be labeled as needing a man. Masculine supremacy and feministic movements both play a significant role in deterring Singles from seeking marriage.

Faithless Views

Some Singles aren't in a rush to marry because they have witnessed so many failed marriages. For instance, Singles who are children of divorces may have trust issues with love, and thus continuously hold off tying the knot. Let's face it, marriage is highly desired, bit isn't highly respected. Isn't that strange? It's disheartening to know there are tons of Singles who believe in and have a desire for a lifetime union, but are hesitant to make such a commitment. They avoid marriage because all of the ones they've seen or experienced have resulted in brokenness and discord.

Casual Romances
There is a deceptive pleasure in finding someone new whenever the desire surfaces. In our society, casual flings with random strangers are encouraged, and more Singles seem to never mature past this "no strings attached" mentality. With apps that are aimed at hooking people up, it makes it even easier for temporary and meaningless connections to occur. The more that Singles engage in casual affairs, the further we will drive ourselves away from a love keeping covenant.

Living Arrangements
Cohabitation is increasing because Singles feel that they can get all the benefits of marriage without actually being in a committed marriage. As more Singles continue to embrace this lifestyle, the more marriage will be put on the back burner. When "shacking up" becomes a way of life, it's hard for Sin-

gles who are used to cohabitating with their significant others to disengage and live apart until they actually decide to marry. Many have already purchased a home, started a family, and are in a place of contentment, and have no regard for matrimony.

> ## "Cohabitation is increasing because Singles feel that they can get all the benefits of marriage without actually being in a committed marriage."

Sharing a home with a significant other isn't the only living arrangement increasing in modern times. Singles between the ages of 18-34 are prioritizing living with their parents over marriage. According to the Pew Research Center, more than a third of the Millennial population is still living at home. Whether it's for financial reasons or because of the familiarity that it brings, many Singles are taking their time leaving the nest.

Mass Incarceration
According to the NAACP fact sheet, America is 5% of the world's population but has 25% of the world's inmates. Yes, one in every four humans in the world is

incarcerated in the United States. Talk about Land of the Free, right? I'm aware that every man or woman that is incarcerated isn't Single, but a significant portion is. With well over two million people in prison today, one can easily see how this impacts the number of marriages. While I agree that justice must be served when a crime is committed, I'm against drawn out sentences (especially for nonviolent crimes) that keep people from entering back into society as functional citizens. This is undeniably impacting Singles from marrying because some potential spouses may be inmates.

WAITING FOR A BETTER REASON

First things first, Singleness is not synonymous with dating. Once you understand this, it will liberate you. I say this because common culture believes that every Single is in some desperate search for a spouse or at very least, looking for a significant other to fill their void. Although this may be true for some, it does not apply to every Single. I want to debunk this myth because its underlying tone implies that being a Single man or woman isn't enough. Even more, it suggests that God isn't enough, and we should know this is very far from the truth. He is the True Lover of our souls and is the only One who can and will make us complete. It's critical that Singles are reminded of our sole dependence on Him, especially when society is trying to redefine us by our relationship status.

"Singleness is not synonymous with dating."

I've struggled at times wondering if God would ever bless me for waiting. Will I ever be married? Will I ever have children? Will I ever become a family man? These are questions I've tussled with. I don't know the answers to any of these questions, but I hope they all will be yes. Psalm 37:4 says, "Delight yourself in the LORD, and he will give you the desires of your heart." Prayerfully, the satisfaction that we put in Christ will lead us to the spouse that we desire to have, but there must be a genuine delight in Him and not happiness for the sole purpose of receiving a spouse. More and more, I feel that it's important for Singles to understand what it means to truly wait.

Waiting is about developing a closer relationship with God while having a confident expectation of His perfect timing for our lives. When we wait, we express complete dependence on His will and totally surrender ours. We should not be waiting on God for a spouse more than we are waiting on God for God. For the Singles who strongly desire marriage, waiting can seem like forever and a day. Is it easy to wait? No. Is it possible? Absolutely. In this season of your life, the focus should be on Christ revealing as much of

Himself to you while you're Single, and looking for Him to satisfy your soul during the process of waiting. Psalm 27:14 says, "Wait for the LORD; be strong and let your heart take courage; yes, wait for the LORD."

> ## "We should not be waiting on God for a spouse more than we are waiting on God for God."

As you wait, focus on becoming the type of godly Single that attracts another godly Single. The desire to be married must be honored with a righteous passion. God is more concerned with your holiness than your happiness. But, when He can see that your true happiness is in Him, and it's an unwavering joy, He is willing to honor a holy union that's for Him. God wants you to be holy forever with Him before He wants you to be happily ever after with them. Honor this season of your Singleness by using this time of waiting as a time of preparation. If we lose sight of Christ in the midst of our feelings, we'll find ourselves in situations that we don't need to be in. The next chapter is a prime example of how I allowed the weight of the wait to influence me.

LONELINESS PARANOIA

When I talk to Singles about their fear of being by themselves, I try to get them to understand the difference between being alone and being lonely. If we are going to wait, we might as well grow, too. Since time is going by regardless, we would be foolish to waste it by dwelling on who we do or do not have in our lives. If another individual can solve our loneliness, why are there Singles who still feel lonely in relationships? Even more, why are there spouses who feel lonely in marriages? Loneliness isn't just based on not having a relationship. More importantly, it's based on the lack of a relationship with God. This is why having time to yourself is critical.

Loneliness is a state of mind. Aloneness is a state of being. Loneliness runs from. Aloneness runs to. Loneliness breeds bitterness, doubt, impatience, and pride. Aloneness produces calmness, contentment, focus, and humility. Loneliness reminds you that someone is absent. Aloneness affirms you that God is present. Loneliness gives a life-doesn't-begin-until-I'm-married mindset. Aloneness gives a life-is-complete-with-Christ mentality. Loneliness is a spiritual disconnection. Aloneness is the opportunity to connect spiritually. Loneliness is the number one identifier of discontentment. Aloneness gives the right attitude for solitude and produces the right attitude for gratitude. Loneliness is suffering from the reality of being by ourselves. Aloneness is experiencing the reality of God's presence. We can be alone and not feel lonely.

When I speak of being alone, I'm speaking about the benefit of being with God, not just a physical state of separation from others or someone. God is always with us, and we should fully embrace Him with the intent of getting to know Him more deeply and more intimately. In John 16:32, Jesus speaks about aloneness to His disciples when He says, "A time is coming and in fact has come when you will be scattered, each to your own home. You will leave me all alone. Yet I am not alone, for my Father is with me." This is a prime example of Jesus being alone in the natural, but never alone in the Spirit with God. The next time you feel yourself battling with feelings of loneliness, use that as an opportunity to redirect your focus from yourself to God and allow Him to minister to you in that moment.

GIVING IN TO LONELINESS

A couple of years ago, my close friend, Justin, and I decided to spend our birthdays in Los Angeles. As much as I love my city of Cleveland, it's always great when I can escape during the cold winter months and bask in warmer weather. I was also excited to visit the west coast for the first time and looked forward to catching up with a young woman I knew from my college days. Let's just say her name is Angel. She relocated to LA for work, and we thought it would be great to go out for dinner while I was in town.

Let me backtrack and give you a little background about this situation. A couple months before I headed to LA, Angel started reaching out to me occasionally via text message. It was awkward at first because she had recently gotten engaged. I knew this because her proposal went viral all over the Internet. Initially, she would text me to randomly check in on me, but soon she started asking me for prayer. After awhile I could sense that something was wrong, and eventually she revealed to me that her fiancé called off the wedding. I felt so bad for her. I could not begin to imagine the embarrassment and humiliation that she had to face on a daily basis from family, friends, and colleagues. I decided to keep in touch with her during this process, and that ultimately led to us talking more frequently.

Okay, fast-forward two months. Justin and I are at a restaurant on Hollywood Boulevard waiting for Angel to arrive. After a few minutes, I felt a tap on my shoulder, and when I turned around, there she stood looking as beautiful as I remembered. We hadn't seen each other since our college days, so we were both glad to finally reconnect in person. That night, the three of us conversed for hours. It felt just like old times. Towards the end of our time together,

Angel invited us to church, and Justin and I agreed to join her there the next morning.

Following service, we decided to grab lunch a Vietnamese Restaurant. After ordering our food, we began to recap the sermon we'd heard that morning. About 15 minutes into our conversation, the server approached the table with our food. As he tried to simultaneously place two bowls of soup on the table, he accidently spilled one on Angel's lap. Everyone's jaws dropped in the restaurant. But to my surprise, she was very calm and polite with the server. As he apologized a million times, Angel graciously pardoned him and told him it was okay. There wasn't even a hint of anger from her. She went to the bathroom and tried her best to dry off. Justin and I were impressed with her kindness and patience. It made me look at her differently, and I mean that in a good way. From that moment on, the vibe between the two of us shifted. After she had changed her clothes, we hung out for the rest of the day.

That night we went for a long walk. As we strolled down the boardwalk, we cracked jokes, laughed, and talked about any and everything. The conversation was going great, and before you know it, we began to express our interest in each other. It seemed so right, but in the back of my mind, I knew how vulnerable we both were. My emotions said yes, but my Spirit said no. I was caught up in the possibility of what could be. When I got back to my hotel, I reflected on how two people who met in their late teens could reconnect in their late twenties. Surely this was fate, right? Life definitely offers some interesting twists and turns. I was confident that we would build from that point on.

Angel and I saw each other every day for the remainder of my time in LA. I honestly didn't want to leave. When I got back to Cleveland, we didn't miss a beat. We sent text messages to each other all throughout the day and talked throughout the night. Although I was fully aware that she had just gotten out of a serious relationship and needed time to heal, I also knew what I "felt." I respected the woman that she was, and I believed that together we could work through her pain. My intentions were pure, but the timing was completely wrong. I was going out of turn. All because of a few great memories and intense feelings, I was ready to move forward with a heartbroken woman.

The connection that I hoped would lead to a relationship eventually ended within a few months. It wasn't like we had a falling out or did something to hurt each other. We just knew that a relationship at that point wasn't in our best interest and we slowly stopped communicating with each other. I had allowed my self-centeredness to interfere with what God was telling me, and I knew better than that. As disappointing as it was, I knew that us disengaging from each other was the best thing for both of us.

I'm sure you want to know why I would put myself in a situation like that, especially when I knew that God was telling me no? The answer: loneliness paranoia. All the pressure that derived from the weight of the wait began to cloud my better judgment, and as soon as an opportunity for a relationship came about I reacted too early. In this chapter, we will discuss loneliness and how it leads to ungodly outcomes; the difference between being alone and being lonely; and what we can do to overcome these feelings of anxiety.

FEAR OF BEING BY YOURSELF

It's one thing to feel loneliness, but it's another to fear loneliness, and that's exactly what loneliness paranoia is. Loneliness paranoia is the fear of being by yourself. Generally speaking, Singles are afraid of the possibility of going through life without a spouse. The majority of us hope to be husbands or wives and it's natural to desire marriage. There is absolutely nothing wrong with Singles wanting to be a spouse. At some point, being the bridesmaid or groomsman begins to weigh on your conscious.

If you search deep into the heart of a Single who struggles with this fear, you will discover that at the very core of their loneliness lies a spiritual disconnection. Before Angel and I reconnected, I was already struggling with wanting to be with someone. As I mentioned in the previous chapter, the pressures that I experienced played a significant role in my state of loneliness. This gradually shifted my focus from having an intimate relationship with Christ to a having an intimate relationship with a woman. All I thought about was finding my wife. Looking back in retrospect, I allowed this personal battle to go unchecked. When we allow loneliness to overtake us, we are essentially saying with our actions, emotions and thoughts that God isn't sufficient and that His promises aren't true. Lingering in a state of loneliness hinders the joy of God's presence and continuously welcomes the burden of isolation. If an idle mind is the devil's workshop, an isolated Single is the enemy's playground.

> "If an idle mind is the devil's workshop, an isolated Single is the enemy's playground."

Even more, the state of loneliness that I experienced welcomed a host of negative emotions. Frustration, doubt and unhappiness were daily feelings for me. I felt like I had waited long enough. I had my mind made up that I was going to be in a relationship when the next opportunity presented itself, and that's exactly what I tried to do with Angel. I developed this woe-is-me mindset, which is a form of pride. If allowed, loneliness can become a dwelling place of comfort for sin.

GOING OUT OF TURN

"Antwan, you're going out of turn." As I sat across the table from a married couple that I was having coffee with, the wife pierced my heart with those words, and to this day they've never left me. "Me? Going out of turn? Do you know how patient I've been? You don't know what I've endured while being on this walk," I thought to myself. There was that pride rising up in me again, but deep down I knew that she was right. Even though I wanted to explain every reason why I was not going out of turn, I reluctantly agreed with a head nod. I was growing restless with the process of being Single. It was evident that I wanted to be in a relationship and she exposed my motive in an honest, yet respectful way.

When loneliness became the theme of my life, my mind was constantly geared towards finding someone who could fill that void, even with me being completely aware that no woman could do such a thing. Having a fear of being by yourself really clouds your discernment on situations when you'd otherwise know better. If we're so eager to be with someone to the point where we are willing to go against our better judgment, we're only proving to God that we're not ready for a relationship. Three of the most common signs of knowing if you are going out of turn are when patience, peace, and purity are absent. Let's take a closer look at this.

The lack of patience leads to forcing or rushing into a relationship. Again, I was eager to be with someone. My end goal was to be a husband, and with that in mind, I began moving too fast. Since Angel and I knew each other, I felt that we could expedite the process. The late Dr. Myles Munroe once said, "You are ready to date when you don't need to date."

The lack of peace in the relationship leads to frustration and uncertainty. Angel was in a state of brokenness, I was in a state of loneliness, and God was in a state of quietness. He was not going to approve of a relationship knowing that neither of us was prepared. When God disapproves, He will consistently prick at your heart with conviction until you obey. And do not make the mistake of accepting His silence as approval. Until He undoubtedly says yes, the answer is no or not yet.

The lack of purity in a relationship leads to guilt and shame. Sexual immorality wasn't an issue for Angel and myself because of how far apart we were from each other, but that isn't always the case for other Singles. When the focus is centered on physical attraction, it is destined for destruction. Righteousness cannot be reflected if we allow impurity to be the theme of the relationship.

[Handwritten notes at top: "Why are you single?" and "check your patience, peace, purity daily"]

Antwan Steele

Having the desire to be with someone is completely understandable. Trust me, I get it. But, we must be truthful and ask ourselves if we are motivated by anxiousness, impatience, and lust to be with someone. In this season of waiting, regardless of how lonely we may feel, we cannot cheat the process. Enitan Bereola, author of Gentlewoman, once said, "A focus on getting a guy before a focus on getting God is backward, and you'll probably end up with a god spelled backward." While this quote was specifically geared towards women, its message applies to all: Be Single by decision and not by default. Too many Singles are lonely because their desperation is stronger than their discipline. Let's allow God to be the One who interrupts our season of Singleness, not ourselves.

> "Be Single by decision and not by default. Too many Singles are lonely because their desperation is stronger than their discipline."

SETTLING INSTEAD OF SETTLING DOWN AND WHAT IT CAN LEAD TO

Often times we don't think of loneliness paranoia as a problem that can cause additional problems. When you're afraid of being lonely, it can tempt you to be with someone that you know you shouldn't be with or keep you in a relationship longer than you should. These are different ways of wrongfully settling instead of rightfully settling down, and many Singles can relate to these struggles. Even worse, in many cases, cohabitation is the end result. Sadly, Singles are compromising by jumping into or holding onto relationships, which speak to a deeper issue that is affecting their value. Since we've already discussed being with someone that we know we shouldn't be with, in other words going out of turn, let's talk about staying with someone longer than we should.

Have you ever stayed in a relationship past its expiration date? Maybe you're currently in a relationship that you know that you should leave, but for whatever reason, you continue to hold on by the thinnest string of false hope. Although it was hard for me to let go of my situation with Angel, I knew that if we continued on, it would become more difficult to end the relationship in the long run. It's always tough to let go of someone that you're interested in, have deep feelings for or even love, especially if you're driven by loneliness. But just as Ecclesiastes 3:6 says, "There is a time to search and a time to quit searching. A time to keep and a time to throw away." The hurtful truth is that some relationships must be thrown away. It doesn't matter how long or how much history you have with someone, holding on to nothing is only hurting you both. Longevity doesn't legitimize love. When you can't let go of who God didn't send, you're prolonging who God wants to bring into your life. Stop allowing loneliness to lie to you and free yourself from the bondage. It's better to be alone and hopeful than to be in a relationship and hopeless.

> ## "It's better to be alone and hopeful than to be in a relationship and hopeless."

There is also the issue of cohabitation. The Single man or woman battles with loneliness, which causes them to go out of turn. This can lead to a premature relationship. But, out of the fear of being lonely, they stay in the relationship, which eventually could result in cohabitation, but no marriage. Again, this is the potential, not always the case.

A fear of loneliness can sometimes lead to the issue of cohabitation. Singles often engage in premature relationships because they simply don't want to be alone. When the feelings of loneliness are so strong that you need someone to be around at all times, cohabitation may be the next step. While it may seem like a good idea to really get to know someone by living with them before marriage, it can lead to multitude of problems and should be avoided.

To be clear, if there is nothing immoral taking place, there is ultimately nothing wrong with a Single man and woman living in the same house, but this is rarely the case. It is hard to remain morally pure when you are attracted to another individual and are able to be with them in the privacy of your home together. Sex before marriage is a sin that is continuously condemned in the Bible and living under the same roof provides ample opportunity for temptation in the area of sexual immorality. God wants us to flee immorality, not knowingly run towards temptation. I'll discuss this in more detail in the next chapter. Another reason why cohabitation should be avoided is because the Bible commands us to avoid the appearance of sin. Thessalonians 5:22 says, "Abstain from all appearance of evil." Two Singles living together are assumed to be sleeping together, even if they are not. While this assumption may seem unfair to you, it is the reality of things and we must take this into consideration. As Believers, it is our responsibility to be clear examples of what is right and not to cause others to stumble or be offended.

Some may be quick to challenge me, so think about it from this standpoint. If two unmarried Singles stay together for sufficient amount of time, they will be tempted to have sex, which can lead to the birth children. At very best, sons and daughters, mothers and fathers, but no husbands and wives will occupy this cohabitated home if they never marry.

Children naturally imitate what their parents do, and if a child grows up seeing their parents live together with no biblical commitment, how do we expect them to honor the union of marriage when they get older? This perpetuates a cycle of Singles opposing the responsibility of marriage, but reaping the benefits of it. If a Single man and woman want to portray an image of a family, the godly way of doing so requires marriage.

According to the Center for Disease Control and Prevention, 48% of women between the ages of 15-44 cohabitated between 2006-2010 as a first union instead of marriage. I would greatly assume that majority of these cohabitating relationships had to do with the fear of being lonely. My point in stating this is to show how a simple feeling of loneliness can lead to a life of unrighteousness, even when it is perceived by society as common or acceptable. Don't let the norms of society cause you to settle for something that is unacceptable in God's sight.

If you want to know if you're settling, here are fifteen signs in no particular order.

1. You put them before God or vice versa
2. You two cannot stop having sex or don't care to stop
3. You live with your significant other even though you know it's wrong
4. You have been with them for years, yet there is no sign of marriage

5. You feel like your partner is stunting your growth

6. You justify your serious concerns about them

7. You don't want to start over with someone new

8. You feel that the relationship is one-sided in effort

9. You are being abused in any aspect

10. You don't believe that God has His best for you

11. You are waiting for them to change

12. You want to leave, but you are afraid to be alone

13. You believe that he or she isn't faithful

14. You two share extremely different values

15. You feel worthless with them and believe that you aren't worth better

I thank God my loneliness didn't allow me to fall neck deep into a situation with Angel that I couldn't get myself out of. Unfortunately, many Singles are stuck in this position, but God is still gracious. There's a difference between settling and settling down. Don't settle unless it's settled in your spirit.

> "There's a difference between settling and settling down. Don't settle unless it's settled in your spirit."

CONTENTMENT BEFORE COMMITMENT

Once the FaceTime, phone calls, and text messages eventually ceased between Angel and me, the frustrating state of loneliness paranoia crept back in. Truthfully, it was never gone; it was nicely disguised in my premature pursuits. However, this is where I learned the importance of contentment before commitment. I realized that it didn't matter who came into my life if loneliness was going to continue to dominate my heart. I couldn't truly receive the woman that God has for me if I placed my value in her, and not in the God that I serve. I had to reach a point where I no longer allowed my joy and peace to be determined or dictated by a relationship. My setback catapulted me into the presence of God's embrace, and that is where I know that I can always rest in unwavering satisfaction.

My all time favorite Scripture is James 1:2-3 where it says, "Consider it pure joy, my brothers and sisters, whenever you face trials of many kinds because you know that the testing of your faith produces perseverance." You may be thinking, how can I consider my feelings of loneliness as pure joy or why would I even want to do such a thing? Sometimes we don't understand why we may still be Single, but what if God was keeping you in this particular season to spiritually mature you? We learn our most meaningful lessons in the trials of our lives than we do in the triumphs of our lives. Being Single is an opportunity to strengthen your faith in Christ so that you can develop endurance that will prepare you for what is to come. Being by yourself is the chance to take your discontentment and turn it into contentment because it will be difficult to know if you're truly satisfied in Christ when other variables are satisfying you before Him.

Furthermore, I believe Romans 8:28 when it says, "And we know that in all things God works for the good of those who love him, who have been called according to his purpose." I had to stop worrying and start trusting. Singles who put their faith in Christ must rest in the truth that God is working it out for our good. The Scripture doesn't say some things, it says all things, and we must know that He is laboring for our benefit. Let me also say that this verse doesn't mean God will grant any and every Single a spouse. Everyone won't be married, but everyone is meant to be content. Knowing that it's all working out according to His will is sufficient because we trust His sovereignty.

Psalm 73:25 says, "Whom have I in heaven but You? And besides You, I desire nothing on earth." Whenever I read this Scripture, I immediately reevaluate where I stand with Christ. I believe it speaks to true contentment. How many Singles you know can repeat this verse and genuinely mean it with all their heart? I'm not talking about just being able to cope with your loneliness, but being able to joyfully embrace Christ in your Singleness. Do you feel that Christ is all you truly need in this life? Do you actually desire Him more than anything on God's green Earth? We have to center our heart's affection on Christ and allow Him to be the one to fulfill the longing in our souls. When God is intentionally cherished and recognized as our Supreme Being, He will reveal more of Himself to us, resulting in true fulfillment.

Considering it pure joy to be in this season. Trust that it's all working for your good, and know that consistently setting your heart on God will lead to contentment. Sure, many Scriptures can be used, but the three that I have just shared with you have blessed me over the years. Memorize them and meditate on them until they become a reality in your inward being and begin to reflect in your outward actions. Ask yourself this question on a regular basis: If God never gives me a spouse, will I still love Him?

LET'S TALK ABOUT SEX

After a few pickup games at an open gym, some of the guys and I decided to grab a bite to eat. While at the restaurant, we talked about everything from sports to family and from business to relationships. "Yo Twan, you still going strong?" One of the guys asked. "Yes sir," I replied. Some of the other guys at the table were curious to know what we were talking about. You should have seen the look on their faces when I told them that I was waiting until marriage to have sex; it was like I had said something completely off the wall. Well, I guess it was bizarre to them seeing as though we live in a world where everything is over-sexualized, and most people view sex as casual and meaningless.

The reasons that we look at sex the way that we do is because it saturates conversations, is promoted in movies, bragged about in songs, used as marketing ploys to entice customers, written about in novels, stamped on billboards, printed in magazines, exploited on television and dominates the Internet. Sex is everywhere, and it's usually celebrated. We don't even realize the consequences of premarital sex because society makes it acceptable and justifiable. It seems like the only time that sex is possibly looked down upon is when someone isn't practicing safe sex.

> "We don't even realize the consequences of premarital sex because society makes it justifiable and acceptable."

As a Single man, I understand the struggles with sexual purity. Abstaining from sexual pleasures until matrimony seems like an impossible journey, but it can be done. Know that God is completely able to deliver you from sexual immorality, but you have to abide by His Word because your deliverance is in your obedience. If He did it for me, I know He can do if for you. Let's discuss our struggles more deeply and see how our flesh, lust, and temptations can lead us to sexual sin. Also, let's observe some of the consequences that stem from premarital sex, the serious issues with pornography, and how we can overcome our sexual battles.

INHERENTLY SINFUL

When God formed Adam and Eve, they were made with perfection. Not one thing about them was flawed. Their skin, organs, and bones were the healthiest of any other human being created. They were intricately designed from the inside out to last forever. Nonetheless, our flesh is made up of a physical and sensual body functioning as an individual; it has needs that must be met for it to be sustained. For example, when we're hungry, we eat. When we're sleepy, we sleep. These are just some of the ways we satisfy or respond to our flesh.

However, when Adam and Eve disobeyed God's command, sin entered the world and tainted man's flesh. Now that sin is in the world, our flesh, which was once just the physical and sensual makeup of man, now becomes our sinful nature. This is what Romans 5:12 means when it says, "When Adam sinned, sin entered the world. Adam's sin brought death, so death spread to everyone, for everyone sinned." Our sinful nature desires to please itself. We were born in sin, and it's our instinct. The affections and cravings of our flesh inevitably violate anything of God and are completely dominated by wickedness. This is why Romans 7:18 says, "In my flesh dwell no good thing." Our natural inclination is to rebel against the will of God and fulfill the desires of our flesh. Nothing pleasing to God can come from the flesh, no matter how appealing and pleasant it may seem. Our sinful flesh has perpetuated from generation to generation, from ancient days to modern times.

Consequently, sin is embedded in the core of our very being, and there is no hope for any Single who attempts to tame it on their own. Once Christ has been accepted as Lord and Savior, the Holy Spirit immediately indwells us. At that time, the battle of the flesh and Spirit will continuously wage war against one another. Our sinful nature craves impulsively to be satisfied while our Spirit patiently desires to be glorified. The sinful nature we embody is hostile to God and constantly tempts us to disobey His commands. One of the main ways that we have been enticed since the beginning of time is through our inherent urge for sexual intimacy stimulated by the evil four-letter word, lust.

SEXUALLY LUSTFUL

In the context of this chapter, lust is an uncontrolled passion for sexual fulfillment outside of marriage that manifests in our actions and thoughts. Since our flesh has been corrupted by sin, it desires what is contrary to God, and lust is the promoter of that satisfaction. Sexual lust is a widespread issue amongst the Single community and needs to be seen for what it truly is because it's in total conflict to the holy standard of God. Many Singles don't want to give up their lustful desires because they love the pleasure of sex even though it's sinful. We don't see how damaging lust is because Satan does a great job at disguising it's destructiveness.

Lust appears to be valuable, but is worthless. Lust is about selfishness. Lust, from the standpoint of sexuality, initiates the problems of fornication, adul-

LET'S TALK ABOUT SEX

tery, pornography, masturbation, four play, oral sex, carnal thoughts and any other sexual activities. The power of lust promises you everything and gives you absolutely nothing. Imagine if you were in a relationship with someone who made guarantees, but never fulfilled any of what was promised. In fact, after getting what they wanted from you, they disappeared. That is what lust does every time. It leads to temporary satisfaction, but offers no lasting gratification. It takes, but never gives. It feels right, but is always wrong. It appears to be authentic, but has proven to be counterfeit. It's full of greed and idolatry. Nothing of virtue comes from lust, and we must do away with it at all costs.

Singles who engage in lust are saying that their wants are more important than God's commands. Sex was designed to consummate the marital bond between husband and wife, but lust completely disregards God's purpose for its own selfish gain. Lust needs to be destroyed, not deployed. Lust leads to sin that takes you farther than you wanted to go, keeps you longer than you wanted to stay, and makes you pay the price larger than you wanted to pay.

> ## "Lust needs to be destroyed, not deployed."

A SEXY INVITATION

Those of us who've accepted Christ as Lord and Savior have been delivered from the penalty of sin, are being delivered from the power of sin and will be delivered from the presence of sin. This simply means that we are saved from the price of sin, which is death. We are being set apart from the influence of sin, which is sanctification. But as long as we live in this evil world, we'll have to deal with the existence of sin. What makes it hard is the attraction of sin also known as temptation, which is an offer from the enemy or your flesh to fulfill ungodly desires at the expense of displeasing God.

Satan is always tempting Singles to fall short. He knows that God has created us with a sexual desire because sex itself isn't sinful. However, the enemy also knows that Singles are prohibited from indulging in sexual pleasure until they've become husband and wife, and this is where the enemy wants us to cross that boundary. God doesn't delight in denying you of sexual pleasure, but He wants it to be preserved until it's honored in the way that it was originally intended. When a man and woman is under the covenant of marriage and engages in sexual intercourse, it becomes an act of worship to God. Satan wants to pervert that. He sees something that is meant to be beautiful and tries to redefine it for those of us who aren't married because he hates anything that glorifies God. Having sex outside of marriage may feel good to us, but it's actually more satisfying to Satan because it's a disgrace to God and detrimental to our soul.

We all have days where we may be feeling more sexual than usual, and Satan knows this and will use temptation to bait us. Because he is persistent and relentless, Satan never stops sending invitations to your flesh to join the party with lust. He will even invade your personal space. Just because temptation knocks at the door of your heart doesn't mean that you have to answer. You have the ability to turn away from temptation. To be tempted is not a sin, but you are responsible for the way that you react to these sexual callings. James 1:13 says, "When tempted, no one should say, 'God is tempting me.' For God cannot be tempted by evil, nor does he tempt anyone; but each person is tempted when they are dragged away by their own evil desire and enticed." Don't allow the lust of the flesh to lure you away from righteousness.

> **"Just because temptation knocks at the door of your heart doesn't mean that you have to answer."**

Furthermore, please understand that temptation becomes stronger the more that you entertain it. Satan will plant seeds of deception in your mind that make you question if what you're about to do is really that bad. This is the same way he tempted Eve in the garden. He'll make you think that sex is okay. He'll make you think that you'll be better off if you do it. He'll make you think that God won't be that disappointed. Dwelling on the thoughts of fulfilling the sexual desires of your flesh makes you even more vulnerable. If you allow the lies to linger in your mind, they'll soon cloud your judgment and override your decision-making ability to remain in God's will, and you'll eventually indulge in sexual immorality.

We have to think about the many escapes God provides for us before we even fall to sexual temptation. 1 Corinthians 10:13 says, "No temptation has overtaken you except what is common to mankind. And God is faithful; he will not let you be tempted beyond what you can bear. But when you are tempted, he will also provide a way out so that you can endure it." Each time that you feel tempted by Satan and your flesh, look for your way out. As I mentioned before, being tempted isn't a sin, but rather an opportunity for us to honor God, which draws us closer to Him through obedience.

SILENT AND SNEAKY SIN

Pornography addiction is problematic in the lives of Believers and unbelievers, and in both men and women. Never in the history of human existence has there been a wider spread attack of pornography on our lives than it is today. We live in the digital era where the Internet is a way of life. A couple decades ago, purchasing a magazine or ordering from a blocked channel on television required individuals to do more work to access pornography. While still possible to reach, these barriers limited the involvement in this sin. However, in modern technological times, pornography has become more readily available, producing record-breaking usage and generating billions of dollars. Pornography is now its own industry and is considered big business.

Because it is so easily accessible and often requires no other bodies outside of one's self, Singles are getting hooked on pornography and masturbation. It is the sin that can be indulged in, without anyone ever finding out, in the comforts of one's own home. So, how are porn and masturbation classified as sins if they are usually done alone and do not involve premarital sex with another person? Any activity that requires one to sin in order to engage in it or inevitably leads one to sin, is consequently a sin itself. Watching porn certainly results in lustful thoughts, while masturbation is fueled by lustful thoughts. Either way, when you really think about it, self pleasure still requires someone else.

Although extremely common, pornography is highly ridiculed, especially in the church where many Believers are struggling with it. If you're caught or heard to be engaging in pornographic activity, you may experience others looking down at you. The typical view of this issue is that a person is perverted or nasty. With that perspective lingering in the atmosphere, it makes it hard for people to come clean about this dreadful captivity. It creates guilt, shame, and worthlessness in oneself, which forces individuals to keep it to themselves, and extends this vicious cycle. And because pornography is a sin that can easily be kept a secret, many Singles remain living in bondage.

> "Singles who battle with porn must understand they're enslaving their future spouse's beauty to false representations they visualize in the present."

Singles who battle with porn must understand they're enslaving their future spouse's beauty to false representations they visualize in the present. In other words, the more you watch porn, the unhealthier your attraction and sexual expectations will be for a future spouse. The images presented in porn are dramatized in order to appeal to our deepest and darkest fantasies. Those who work in the porn industry are good at making their photographs and videos come off as extremely euphoric and pleasurable to get and keep you hooked. Ultimately, porn is a lie. There is nothing wrong with wanting an attractive spouse and desiring a great sex life, but if it's motivated by the things seen in porn, you're setting your future marriage up for potential failure.

CONSEQUENTIAL EFFECTS

I don't think we truly realize how sexual immorality affects not just us as individuals, but also our relationships, families, communities, and our society as a whole. Our culture highlights the pleasures of sexual immorality but turns a blind eye to its ravaging outcomes. We as Singles need to accept that sexual sin may feel good to us, but sex is not meant for us in this season. I know this may not be the most received message, but it's the truth. We are ruining each other's lives over short-lived sexual fulfillment.

> "Our culture highlights the pleasures of sexual immorality, but turns a blind eye to its ravaging outcomes."

Sex outside of marriage has resulted in abortions, children born out of wedlock, future impact on marriages, physical harm, emotional suffering, relational damage and spiritual separation. When sex results in an estimated 3,000 babies being aborted daily in the United States, and well over half of these abortions coming from unmarried women in their 20s, there's a problem. When sex leads to broken homes where the child suffers, there's a problem. When sex and porn addiction results in the devaluing of a future covenant between a husband and wife, there's a problem. When sex results in millions of Singles contracting STDs, whether curable or incurable, there's a problem. When sex leads to guilt, shame, worthlessness, and a host of other negative feelings, there's a problem. When sex and porn lead to shattered relationships, there's a problem. When sex and porn creates a widening gap between God and us, there's a problem. In other words, having sex outside of marriage and engaging in pornographic activity only leads to problems. Nothing good comes from premarital sex or pornographic activity but a temporary high and some ungodly outcomes, regardless if they're immediate or prolonged. Like my Pastor says, "satisfied flesh is always sorry."

PERSONAL TESTIMONY TO BATTLING SEXUAL SIN

I was undeniably a mess in my late teens and early 20s. Before my own salvation, I engaged in sexual sin with little to no remorse for my actions. I had zero regards for women or their feelings. I was full of lustfulness, and my focus was solely on satisfying my fleshly desires. I manipulated situations to get what I wanted and did it over and over again. If she was attractive, I was trying to have sex with her. But once I got into a relationship, I stopped sleeping around with multiple women. As I mentioned in the first chapter, I thought I was doing the right thing by having sex with only one woman. I believed that I was "faithful." I later understood that my sexual involvement with one woman was just as wrong as sex with multiple women because I was unmarried. I was still being unfaithful to God, to say the least.

This is nothing that I'm proud of, and from time to time, I have to fight the thoughts of guilt whenever the enemy tries to remind me of my past. I share this part of my life with you in hopes of you seeing how great God's grace and mercy is and how far He's brought me along. Prayerfully, it will encourage you. Once I surrendered my life to Christ, I was given new heart affections to live for Him. God began the process of conditioning my mind from all that I thought was cool or right. This didn't mean that my sexual desires went away, but that I now had the power of the Holy Spirit to overcome sexual sin. Because fornication was such a common sin in my life, it meant and still means a lot to me to stay pure. Here are some practical reminders that have helped me in my battle against sexual sin:

Humble Confession

It can be hard to openly admit that you struggle with any type of sexual sin. Confessing your sin before God brings forth forgiveness. This is very much needed because the only sin that can be overcome is a sin that has been forgiven. 1 John 1:9 says, "If we confess our sins, He is faithful and righteous to forgive us our sins and to cleanse us from all unrighteousness." The Bible says all unrighteousness, not some unrighteousness. Let God purify your heart from this wickedness. Also, there's a need to confess your struggles to someone you trust that'll be able to help you. The purpose of confessing sin to one another is so that we can be healed and held accountable. Don't allow pride to keep you from admitting your shortcomings. Humility precedes honor. God is compassionate with those who humble themselves and own their sin. Proverbs 28:13 says, "People who conceal their sins will not prosper, but if they confess and turn from them, they will receive mercy." Confessing to God and others shouldn't be a one-time thing. Until you've overcome this sin, your confessions should be ongoing because it keeps you humble. When you confess, don't spare any details. The truth shall set you free.

Accountable Friends

Singles love their privacy, and it's natural to keep our struggles a secret in fear of being judged or appearing weak. Regardless of how you feel, it is important to have trusted friends who are there to correct you with truth, encourage in faith, rebuke in love, and teach with wisdom. Accountability is a major step to overcoming sexual immorality. Don't underestimate the power of community. It's difficult to be beaten by the enemy when other Believers always surround you. If you're hesitant about having accountability partners, you run the risk of falling. The enemy is eager to attack us when we're isolated. Having someone to call in the midnight hour to pray with or having weekly recaps is needed. You do not need someone who's passive or so busy that they can't follow up. Having friends who'll be there when you call is nice, but you need someone who's going to be persistent, nosey, and will press you for the sake of holiness. While having friends who are reactive is good, it's even better to surround yourself with friends who'll be proactive in your fight for purity.

Rather Be Wise Than Be Strong

This motto has been a helpful reminder throughout my tender years of Singleness, and it's kept me from the bed of sexual immorality. Wisdom always tells you to avoid, flee, and resist lustful temptations, not test your strength by hanging around to see if you can endure. 1 Corinthians 6:18 says, "Flee from sexual immorality." A huge mistake that many of us make is thinking that we can stand against the callings of our flesh. In some cases, we can. But for the most part, we can't, and we shouldn't try. Overcoming sexual sin is about fleeing and resisting, not staying and fighting. Our flesh is the addiction, lust is the drug, temptation is the means, and sin is the high. Lust and temptation work together with our flesh to carry out sin, but if we starve our flesh by avoiding temptation, lust won't be relevant, and sin won't occur.

Holiness Over Horniness

1 Thessalonians 4:3-5 says, "God's will is for you to be holy, so stay away from all sexual sin. Then each of you will control his own body and live in holiness and honor, not in lustful passion like the pagans who do not know God and his ways." It's God's will that you be set aside for His honorable use. That is what it means to be holy. God has plans that He wants to exercise through you, but those plans will be hindered if you engage in sexual immorality. I have a sincere desire to do what God has called me to do, and I don't want to allow a moment of pleasure to block the call on my life and break the fellowship that I have with God. Don't allow temporary horniness to stand in the way of your lifetime of holiness.

> "Don't allow temporary horniness to stand in the way of your lifetime of holiness."

Guard Your Heart

What are you listening to? What type of conversation are you joining in? Even more, what are you watching? Proverbs 4:23 says, "Above all else, guard your heart, for everything you do flows from it." A common misconception that Singles tend to believe is that falling short is something that occurs on the spot. No, it's a series of decisions over a period time that leads to shortcomings. If you're feeding your flesh more than you're feeding your spirit, you run the risk of allowing your flesh to choose to engage in activities that are displeasing to God. I've learned to cut out things that give strength to my sinful nature, and instead, I focus on what strengthens my spirit. Protect your heart, especially from sexual images and thoughts. You'll be better for it.

Get Busy Doing Useful Work

It's much harder to engage in sexual sin when you're busy laboring for The Lord. The reason why many Singles fall is because they allow themselves to have too much time to wander. You have to get into the habit of avoiding laziness and other situations that cause sexual vulnerability. Get active by doing something. Read a book, clean your home, cut your grandparent's grass, or serve at your church or in the community. Maybe you have a book in you or a business that you want to start. Whatever it is, get moving. There are days that I'm so focused on the work God has for me to do that temptations are at a minimum. Stay busy, stay pure.

"Stay busy, stay pure."

Savor The Beauty Of God

Every time that a Single man or woman gives into lust, they're saying that Christ alone cannot satisfy them. They'd rather pursue the lies of sexual pleasure than the truth of Christ's sufficiency. I've sinned against God and dishonored His daughters so much in the past, and the fact that He's forgiven me is one of many reasons why I never want to disrespect Him or His creation in that regard again. To know that I'm loved with an everlasting love makes me want to love Him more through obedience. I don't have to be threatened with the horrors of Hell. I can be motivated by the fact that one day, I will get to dwell with my Heavenly Father who's saved me from all the wrong that I've done. His goodness is all we need and will satisfy us as we seek Him with our whole heart, mind, soul, and strength. Be wrapped up in His love. It'll help you resist sexual temptation.

There isn't a one-size-fits-all plan for Singles when it comes to combating sexual sin, but these practical steps have helped me, and I pray that they will help you. It's important that you're diligent about your pursuit of sexual purity. Avoiding the opportunity to sin, focusing on holiness, guarding your heart, maintaining a healthy work ethic, and forever dwelling on the beauty of Christ are sure to keep you free from sexual sin.

> "Every time that a Single man or woman gives into lust, they're saying that Christ alone cannot satisfy them."

CAPTION THIS

What were people doing before social media? I always ask myself this question as if I never grew up in an era when social media wasn't popular. But because social media has had such a significant impact on my life and people in general in the past 10 years, I tend to forget what it was like to not have it at my disposal. In today's time, it has become an advertising, entertainment, and informational hub for business and personal use.

Social media is a global sensation in the 21st century, and its popularity of use has permeated multiple aspects of society. Facebook, Instagram, LinkedIn, Snapchat and Twitter account for well over a billion users, and that doesn't include some of the other social media networks or even the video sharing website, Youtube. With a majority of the population using some form of social media on a daily basis, this phenomenon is bound to have an impact on the lives of Singles. Even though this mainstream method of communication has been a blessing to many, it has been a curse to some as well.

Countless issues can be covered on this topic, but I'll address a few that I feel are most necessary and relevant for Singles. The issue isn't social media; the issue is and has always been us. Our inherently sinful nature exposes our hearts through the overconsumption and mishandling of social media. In my humble opinion, I believe that the root cause of this misuse is our need for false validation. From this, flows all other social media concerns. Let's converse.

THE NEED FOR SOCIAL MEDIA VALIDATION

Before I discuss the social media aspect of being validated, let's look at validation for itself. In a nutshell, to be validated means to prove something as acceptable. To be accepted is one of our deepest desires because it gives us a sense of belonging. Everyone wants to belong because it breeds a feeling of security. Sadly, the world doesn't accept individuals for who they are, and this forces us to look for validation from others, even if it's an insincere sense of acceptance. When the need to be validated and the platform of social media are combined, it can produce a lifestyle motivated by the hope for acceptance from spectators. In other words, you get a bunch of Singles living for the likes of those that they don't know. Many will deny this, but it's the truth. It sounds trivial, but it's a reality.

Posting on social media and then waiting for the responses to fill us up is equivalent to pouring water into a jar with large holes and expecting it to stay full. Because our audience on social media can increase with followers and friends, it drives us to keep giving ourselves to the platform for a return on investment. We invest ourselves and in return, we can reap the reward of validation, which diminishes quickly and entices us to make more investments of ourselves for our audience. Often times, the more friends and followers we have, the more likes and comments we receive, the more validated that we feel. This puts us in the cycle of social media validation.

> **"Posting on social media and then waiting for the responses to fill us up is equivalent to pouring water into a jar with large holes and expecting it to stay full."**

Before you jump down my back, understand that I'm not saying that social media is bad or that validation isn't enjoyable. To be honest, it's encouraging when someone acknowledges something that we posted; it's like a digital high five. However, followers and likes may be looked at as a compliment to your value, but not the definition of your value. If your value is *validated* by a strangers' decision to tap a digital icon, you're in a dangerous place. What we share on social media should always be for God's validation. Galatians 1:10 says, "For am I now seeking the approval of man, or of God? Or am I trying to please man? If I were still trying to please man, I would not be a servant of Christ."

This desire to be validated and accepted by man is nothing new and was problematic long before the Internet or the technology world was imagined. It's a heart issue of pride that we're dealing with. Social media should be used for the glory of God. Instead, it has provided more opportunities to satisfy self through comments, likes, reposts, retweets, shares, subscribers, tags, and views. Until we recognize that our hearts are desperately wicked and desire validation from man and not God, we will continue to abuse the purpose of our social media platforms. It's even causing unauthentic lifestyles amongst Singles. Many are feeding off validation at the expense of deceiving others.

THOU SHALL NOT THIRST TRAP

Thou shall not thirst trap. I think those words are somewhere in the Bible, right after the book of 2 Hesitations. Okay, I'm joking, but the issue of "thirst trapping" is serious. If you don't know what that term means, a thirst trap is slang for when someone posts a seductive picture with the sole intent of getting lustful attention from others, or at least that's how I define it. Social media is flooded with sexually enticing pictures. Instead of speaking against it, we encourage this wickedness with comments like "sexy" or multiple heart eye emojis. I used to think thirst traps were something that only applied to women, but men are also guilty of posting these kind of photos.

Single woman, you're exclusive and precious. No one should know the details of your body, especially just from social media observation. You may do it for attention, but instead you're seeking will attract someone God didn't send. Your girls are writing "sexy", so you're mistaking your behavior as an acceptable. Now, he's putting heart eyes under your photos or sliding in your DM's and you're mistaking this for genuine interest. At some point, you have to realize that those half naked pictures you're posting are the seeds to your heartbreaks. Showing off your behind in skintight dresses or revealing cleavage in low cut shirts, or worse, doesn't represent purity in any form. The social media world celebrates the female body not because they accept her for her, but because they're turned on simply by what they see.

> "At some point, you have to realize that those half naked pictures you're posting are the seeds to your heartbreaks."

Single man, your body is restricted as well. Until social media came around, I didn't realize that men sharing sexual pictures and women lusting over them was such a prevalent issue. If you are a Single man who is thirst trapping, you are seeking attention as well. However, you must know that God isn't sending the wife He has for you while you demean yourself and disgrace the true representation of a man. Posting a picture of yourself that exposes the print of your private area belittles your value to being physical alone. Instead, a man should be valued for his submission to Christ and eventually his godly commitment to his wife and family. Pictures with your shirt off or selfies while wrapped in a towel are enticing and may cause a woman stumble into lustful thoughts or actions. As mentioned before, you have sinned by causing another to sin. Single men must know that the posting of their bodies is only a means for the viewer's pleasure, and it's just as sinful as what Single women do.

Are you content with knowing that your audience only desires you for their own pleasure? Are you okay with misleading others? Why does your bio say God is first, but your pictures say that God is last? It's deceptive and must be stopped. It may seem pleasing to the eye of others at the moment, but you do not want to be the cause of another's falling. Your body has the influence to intoxicate its viewer. This can reap eternal consequences. Luke 17:1 says, "One day

Jesus said to his disciples, "There will always be temptations to sin, but what sorrow awaits the person who does the tempting!" Be modest. Cover up. Honor God, yourself, and others.

DECEPTION OF PERCEPTION

If today, every social media app was banned from society, how would you live your life? Even more, if you are in a relationship, how would it change without the existence of social media? I ask these two questions because I want to address the deceit Singles experience on social media from two perspectives: lifestyle and relationships. They both cover a broad scope of the life of Single men and women because social media culture appeals to the way that we live and the way that we love. But, before we go any further, let's define what the deception of perception is in regards to social media.

Deception occurs when something appears to be true but is false. Perception occurs when you interpret something based on your own point of view. So, in the context of this chapter, the deception of perception would be to appear as someone you're not with the intent of getting friends and followers to view you in a way that you desire. Social media is a playing field for dishonesty because perception allows what we see on these sites to be seen as reality even when it's not a reality. Life can be whatever people make it, even if it's a lie. Let's talk about life-style first.

> "Social media is a playing field for dishonesty because perception is a reality even when it's not a reality."

It's no mystery that social media is a part of our daily activity. We use our photos to highlight the best parts of our lives. Also, with the seamless ability to upload videos on Facebook, Instagram, Snapchat, Twitter, and Youtube, we've become something like stars of our own reality shows. With these platforms at our disposal, we can carefully construct who we want to be to our social media audiences at all times. Sounds cool, right? Yeah, it would be if what we were sharing wasn't contrary to who we are or who we should be.

On top of that, appearance is emphasized by our culture, and social media is the stage where we can show off all that we have or portray ourselves as someone who has a lot. Single men and women get trapped with the desire to maintain or obtain a life-style motivated by what they hope others will be impressed by, but life is more than materialism. Many

Singles will either reduce themselves or never rise to who they truly are because they need to perceive themselves as someone they're not. This results in a deceptive lifestyle. Social media exposes the hearts of those who have many possessions or act like they have many possessions. Both can be detrimental.

"Single men and women get trapped with the desire to maintain or obtain a lifestyle motivated by what they hope others will be impressed by, but life is more than materialism."

Furthermore, relationships are always admired. Everyone loves to see love on display, and there's no foul in that by itself. The problem arises when Single men and women are using their relationships as a ploy to be accepted and be perceived as a perfect couple. You get a bunch of couples hiding behind fake love to appear a particular way to the masses. A Single woman once told me that she'd rather look happy than actually be happy. Relationships have become so commercialized by Singles that it creates a false perception, resulting in thousands, if not millions of deceived Singles. You see Singles posting "relation-ship goals" under someone's picture simply because of what they see. Some couples on social media may be camera-friendly and unhappy, clever posers and miserable, great actors and depressed, good liars and dissatisfied.

This doesn't mean that all relationships are this way, but we have to be careful that we're not posting one thing and living another, or that we're not so consumed by the love life of others that it makes us desire something that may not be true. To be clear, I'm not saying Singles cannot post on social media about their relationship. I'm saying we shouldn't use our relationships to be accepted by others at the ex-pense of deception. For example, don't post about how much you love your man or woman, with the intent of getting a bunch of likes, when you're actual-ly cheating on them.

> Social media can impede on more important things of life, and if we're not aware, it can eat up chunks of our day.

PLEASANT PROPOSALS AND
WONDERFUL WEDDINGS

I was working on a project and hadn't been on social media all day. When I finally got some down time, I decided to open up Instagram. As I scrolled through my timeline, I kept seeing this video of a woman in a black dress crying as she stood in front of a building with an older man. Everyone was snapping pictures and recording her. When I first saw the video, I didn't think much of it because I didn't know the story behind it. As I kept scrolling, I started to see more posts of the same video with the hash tag "Forever Duncan" attached to them. That's when I became curious and sought out the story behind these posts.

The boyfriend surprised his girlfriend with a proposal in front of their family and friends. After his touching speech, he sent her to a hotel to get ready for what she believed to be an evening engagement photo session. There were beauticians and stylists there the moment she walked through the door. After doing her hair and makeup and putting on a beautiful dress, she headed out with her friends. She had no clue what was about to happen. As she was getting out the car, blindfolded and all, she was guided to a door. When they took the blindfold off of her, she saw her father standing next to her and a bunch of people awaiting her arrival. Once she realized what was going on, she began to cry tears of joy as she walked down the aisle. Not only did her boyfriend propose, but he also married her that very same day. She woke up a girlfriend, by noon she was a fiancé, and by the evening she was a wife. This is one of the most inspirational stories that I have ever seen.

As beautiful as it was to witness from a distance such an amazing testimony, I couldn't help but wonder how many Single men and women were going to be impacted by these posts. Social media has become a platform where proposals and weddings are admired. This admiration isn't wrong, however, we can't focus on the proposal more than the engagement or the wedding more than the marriage. If we're not careful, we will be aiming for a day of bliss instead of a lifetime of love. Because everything can be shared instantly, many Singles are consciously or subconsciously preparing themselves for that day where they can be honored as the bride or groom. Yes, that's a great desire, but we have to keep our hearts in check and make sure that we're not moving off of someone else's love story.

"We can't focus on the proposal more than the engagement or the wedding more than the marriage.

CAPTION THIS

Additionally, I must say that the groom in the "Forever Duncan" story definitely raised the bar. However, its crucial to remember that while you may be inspired or encouraged by someone else's story, their story isn't your story. As Single men and women, it's easy to look at what other couples are doing and get lost in the moments they capture. You shouldn't base what God has for you off of what He did for someone else. Don't get caught in the trap of comparison.

Single women aren't the only ones who look forward to these special days, as there are Single men who are just as eager. There are times when I pondered on where I'd propose to my future wife or how she'd look coming down the aisle or what would be the song that we'd have our first dance to. These are natural thoughts for someone who desires marriage and seeing others live it out makes us want it even more, which is totally understandable. However, sometimes it seems like proposals and weddings are used more as entertainment and performances, and less as a way to honor God through a covenant of marriage. It's easy to become superficial before we even make it to that point. Let's honor these stories more loosely and not cherish them too tightly. Again, there's nothing wrong with proposals and weddings. We just have to guard our hearts, especially when we're in a vulnerable state because they can lead us into making decisions driven by emotion.

BREAK FREE FROM DIGITAL DISTRACTIONS

Our carnal nature is easily enticed by the sensations social media has to offer. The more we keep our heads down, gazing at our phones or keep our phones in the air attempting to catch every moment, the more we'll underappreciate life. We've never experienced distractions like this before, but we still have the ability to unplug from the demands of social media and plug into the number one source, which is God. If we truly desire to align with the will of God, we must make time to detach ourselves. Here are some useful ways to mindfully manage our social media use:

Put God First

You probably know the scripture Matthew 6:33, which says "But seek first his kingdom and his righteousness, and all these things will be given to you as well." The context of this verse is affirming us to not worry about the necessities of life such as what we'll eat, drink or wear, but urges us to put Him first. If God is urging us to seek Him before the essentials of survival, social media has to be taken into account as well. When you get up in the morning, do you seek God first or your social media activity? Don't fret, I've been guilty of this as well. From this day forward, commit to a morning devotional that consists of reading your Word and prayer time before you grab your phone and start scrolling. As you progress in consistency, you'll start to see your desire for Christ exceed your interest for what's happening online.

Limit Your Daily Consumption

Throughout the day, I frequently glance at social media. Sometimes, I can literally close out one of the apps before returning for an update only five minutes later. All of the clicking, liking, observing, and scrolling can be very time-consuming. I know, it's sad. In an effort to spend less time on the Internet and more time with God, I've learned to discipline myself to read my Word instead. When I have the urge to hop back on to social media, I remind myself that the time I give to Facebook, Instagram, etc, could be time that I spend more constructively. Social media can impede on more important things of life, and if we're not aware, it can eat up chunks of our day. If your habits are extreme, look into software that allows you to set daily limits, tracks your usage, and even forces you off your phone with alerts. Moment and Offtime are two options. Don't allow social media to become a form of idolatry in your life. Also, remain consistent with your convictions. The Holy Spirit will nudge at your heart if you start to overindulge. We don't want to keep falling short to entertainment gluttony.

Fast From Social Media

Taking an extended break from social media and filling that time with God is also vital. I've noticed that my days are more peaceful and productive when social media is not a part of my daily life. There are different ways to fast. You can do a month, week, or a day's worth of fasting. Sometimes I'll fast from sun up to sun down, one day out of the week, or for an entire week. Whatever you feel led to do, make sure that you use that time to seek His presence. Don't just get off social media and not spend time with God. The point of a fast is to draw closer to Him, not to go on a holy social media strike.

Represent Christ Online

Social media can be great for reuniting families, connecting friends, advertising brands, engaging audiences, and gathering information. There are many ways to use these platforms for our benefit and the benefit of others, but what about the glory of God? More importantly, we can and should use it to spread the Gospel. However, the enemy loves to pervert anything that's meant for good. Our flesh and Spirit fights daily over who should be uplifted: Christ or self? We can point people to Jesus with the light of our lives or turn people away with carnal posts. Always be conscious of who you represent. There's always an audience. Someone is paying very close attention. As followers of Christ, we're expected to represent the Kingdom at all times, and that includes social media as well. Your walk may be the very thing that inspires them to surrender his or her life to Christ. We should not only consider what we post on social media, but also have to be conscious of what we're engaging in, who we're befriending or following, what we're liking and sharing with our online viewers. If we don't monitor all aspects of our intake and usage, we can influence in the wrong way and be influenced in the wrong way. Here are some important questions to ask yourself in regard to social media:

- Do you use social media for validation?
- Do you find yourself comparing?
- Does it make you want to compete?
- Does it make you envious?
- Are you bragging?
- Are you lusting after ungodly images?
- Are you leading people away from God?
- Who do you follow and are they influencing you?
- Do you gossip with friends about what you've seen?
- Does social media pressure you into making rash decisions?
- How many hours a week are you spending on social media?
- Do you seek God before checking your profiles?
- Above all, are you representing Christ online?

Ponder on these questions, be honest with your answers, and then make the necessary adjustments for the better. We should always evaluate how social media is impacting our lives and if we're conducting ourselves in a manner that's pleasing to God. 2 Corinthians 13:5 says, "Examine yourselves to see whether you are in the faith; test yourselves. Do you not realize that Christ Jesus is in you--unless, of course, you fail the test?" All in all, we have to constantly check ourselves to make sure that we're using social media in ways that are truthful and God exalting, not deceptive or self-gratifying.

THIS SEASON'S CALLING

2:30. 2:35. 2:40. 2:45. 2:50. Every five minutes I glanced at the clock with knots in my stomach. I had a one-on-one meeting scheduled with my boss, and she had no idea that I was about to resign. I glanced again at the bottom of my computer screen, and it read 2:55. I went to the bathroom and prayed, then walked over to her office.

She greeted me as I sat down, but continued typing on her computer, barely looking my way. I sat there in silence waiting patiently with my head rested on my folded hands. She then turned to me and said, "What are you doing, praying?" I lifted my head and gave her this blank stare. She leaned back in her seat and said, "You're leaving me huh?" The moment that she spoke those words, tears began to fall down my face. "I'm so sorry, I tried to hold out as long as I could," I said to her. "That's okay, how long are you giving me?", she gracefully asked. I answered, "One month."

It was painful to look her in the eyes and tell her that I was leaving because she had just promoted me to a new position four months before I made this decision. In fact, the raise and promotion that I received were the very things that expedited my leave. I thought if I made more money and had more responsibility that I'd be content. Huge misconception.

When I received both, I still lacked the fulfillment that I longed for because God had something else prepared for me. And, when you go against what He's leading you to do, peace will always be a struggle in your life. I will no longer let a dollar or an opportunity dictate my destiny. No money or position can equate to God's calling for my life.

> "I will no longer let a dollar or an opportunity dictate my destiny. No money or position can equate to God's calling for my life."

You may not be led to leave your job and join ministry full-time, but God is always encouraging us to accomplish His purpose no matter what circumstances we may be in. While you're Single, you have the blessing of doing all that you can in this season of your life for His glory.

In chapter one, we talked about the reason for our existence, which is to know God, love God, and show God. That's the broad scope of the Christian lifestyle and should give Singles the clarity that they need to answer the "why am I here" question. Each one of us is made to labor for God, but often times we feel discouraged, lost, or stressed when it comes to pinpointing our particular part. We tend to settle for the ordinary and rarely consider how we can serve God where we are with the unique abilities that He's given us.

It's sad to say, but callings never get realized in many Singles lives because we just go with the flow and live with no intention of pursuing God's will. As Gospel Artist William McDowell once said in a song, "I don't want to get to Heaven with my life on full. Full of visions unrealized. Full of dreams unrealized." That is exactly what this chapter is about. God has meaningful work for you to accomplish and I want to help you discover what that is. I will use my personal testimony as a reference, and I will walk you through what I have learned with hopes of you gaining an understanding of this season's calling.

RENEWING YOUR MIND

I understand why God didn't give me the vision of this book immediately. I was too anxious and impatient. My job was to seek clarity of His will by trusting that He would reveal what He was calling me to do in His timing, not mines. Going ahead of God was a clear indication that I wasn't ready, and I believed it prolonged the process. In retrospect, there was a particular biblical truth that led to my calling.

Romans 12:2 says, "Do not conform to the pattern of this world, but be transformed by the renewing of your mind. Then you will be able to test and approve what God's will is —His good, pleasing and perfect will." For us to know what God's good, pleasing, and perfect will is, we must deviate from the ways of this world. This means that we cannot be like the world and expect to impact the world. Also, our minds must be refreshed, renewed, and replenished in His Word so that our thinking is transformed for His works.

Our mind doesn't need to be renewed to know that we are called to serve God because this is something that we are already aware of. Our minds need to be renewed to serve Him the way that He specifically calls us to. Every Single man or woman in the Body of Christ has a particular calling. Again, please understand that I'm not saying everyone will have a calling that requires him or her to preach to the nations or start a multi-million dollar business. Your calling could be teaching in schools, preaching in churches, cleaning up communities, feeding the homeless, writing books, etc. Just know that each and every Single has an exclusive call in this season. Renewed minds unlock God's purpose for our lives.

"Renewed minds unlock God's purpose for our lives."

Being transformed by the renewing of your mind comes from filling your mind with the Word of God. The more you feed on His truth, drawing closer to Him, the less you will abide by the errors of the world and be equipped for the work that God has for you. There is no cutting corners or shortcuts, only learning His will and then depending solely on the Holy Spirit to lead you in the right direction. Trust that He will guide you.

TAP INTO YOUR GENIUS

Many Singles are missing out on countless opportunities in life because they have no desire or lack the confidence to seek out their gifts. This is frustrating because it means that far too many Singles are living their lives with untapped potential. Instead of embodying a conquering spirit, their hearts are overcome by doubt, fear, laziness and a host of other obstacles, which results in undeveloped and unexpressed talents and gifts.

Talents are blessings of common grace from God that both Believers and Unbelievers receive. Some talents are developed through hard work and dedication, while others are graced with natural ability that requires hardly any additional training or exposure. Talents aren't necessarily spiritual, but they can and should be used to glorify God. How can one use a talent for the glory of God you ask? Simply by using his or her platform to honor God. If you're a musician, you can glorify God through your talented expression. You wouldn't make music that's contrary to what God commands. Therefore, you would use your talents to exalt His name.

On the other hand, you have spiritual gifts that only Believers are blessed with because the Holy Spirit distributes these gifts. Every Single who is a follower of Christ is graced with spiritual gifting and therefore can never say that they lack in this regard. We don't have to earn our spiritual gift(s), but there can be a lack of effort in finding them. Some examples of gifts would be someone who is graced with the gift of administration, hospitality, mercy, or teaching. While all talents are not necessarily spiritual, all gifts are spiritual and solely purposed in edifying Christ. 1 Corinthians 12 and Romans 12 are two chapters that reference gifts of the spirit. You may even be graced with the ability to lead other Single Christians or organize Christian events for Singles. Whatever it is, it will always move the Kingdom agenda forward.

Talents and spiritual gifts are blessings given from God that express His goodness. There are differences between the two even though they may overlap, but they both should be used for the glory of God. There isn't one specific outline to follow on how to activate what's inside of us, but life experiences, serving people, and confirmation from others all play a role in having a better understanding of what your natural and spiritual abilities are. Even more, it's crucial to pay close attention to what our reoccurring interests are, as they usually go hand and hand with what God has graced us for. Let's take a look.

PASSIONATE PURSUITS

Every Single man or woman has a passion for something. Our allegiance to God determines if that passion is holy or not, and if we're not careful, we'll find ourselves pursuing things God never intended for us to do. This is why it's critical that we seek God's guidance in what He wants us to do. Furthermore, Psalm 37:4 says, "Delight yourself in the LORD; And He will give you the desires of your heart." When your fulfillment is in God, He will fill you with an unwavering yearning that can only be sustained by Him. Our delight in God ignites a passion in us that comes from God. We can be passionate about plenty of things, but when it comes to our calling, we have to go through Him. For the context of this chapter, passion is a deep desire that longs to accomplish the purpose for God.

You'll know that you're passionate about something when you have an increasing awareness about a certain group of people or specific cause. Passion isn't just some great burst of emotion that comes and goes. Passion is the God-given enthusiasm and strength to encourage and sustain you in the accomplishing of your call. But know that whatever longing

God has placed in your heart to accomplish, it will always be to solve a problem for someone else. There is always a need attached to your passion, or better yet, there is always a passion attached to a need. God won't give you a passion for hoarding or for squandering His blessings. He will give you a passion for advancing and edifying His kingdom.

> "Passion isn't just some great burst of emotion that comes and goes. Passion is the God-given enthusiasm and strength to encourage and sustain you in the accomplishing of your call."

Every day won't be filled with enjoyment and excitement, even when you're doing what you're passionate about. That sounds more like Heaven. We have to keep in mind that we live in a fallen world that's corrupted by sin. Our labor will be burdensome at times. We'll have our days when we don't want to use our talents or spiritual gifts to meet the needs of others. Some days we'll be tired, stressed, discouraged, or lonely. I speak from experience. When writing this book, I had moments when I thought about giving up. I had moments when I thought that this wasn't a good idea. I had moments that made me feel like no one believed in me. But, I'm so thankful that my passion came from God alone. I was often times reminded of why this book is important and all of the Singles that it would serve. These are the moments when passion is most important because it helps us endure. Even more, this is why it must come from God.

BRINGING THEM TOGETHER

Sometimes everything that you need to get started is right in front of you. God leaves clues, and if you're paying attention, you'll recognize them. When I look back over the years, I was already serving in Singles ministry at my church because I had a passion for those who were Single. Writing came naturally to me and I had been using this talent to glorify God by sharing brief posts about living as a Christian Single on social media. I also knew God had blessed me with the ability to teach, which is my spiritual gifting. The struggles that Singles were facing was a clear indication there was a need. Everything was pointing me in the direction of what God wanted me to do, which was to write this book. I just needed to be patient and wait for God's guidance. Jeremiah 29:11 says, "For I know the plans I have for you, declares the Lord, plans to prosper you and not to harm you, plans to give you hope and a future." Do you trust His plan?

To make this practical, let me ask you some questions. What are you passionate about? And no, I refuse to accept the typical "I don't know" response. Really think about this. What passions of yours are buried deep inside? What problems would you like to solve in the world? What breaks your heart or continuously frustrates you? How could you go about fulfilling someone else's needs? What talents do you have? What are you good at? And lastly, do you know what the spiritual gifts are in the Bible? If you're not aware, look them up and try cultivating some of the gifts that you feel may be most relevant to you through your local body church. We can't be too relaxed about seeking His will or overly busy doing everything except what He's called us to do, and then become disappointed when we're not fulfilled. Our calling requires a diligent and persistent pursuit.

"We can't be too relaxed about seeking His will or overly busy doing everything except what He's called us to do, and then become disappointed when we're not fulfilled."

Answering the call that God has for you will be a sacrifice. As author John Maxwell says, "When you are bigger than your purpose, that is your career. When your purpose is bigger than you, that is your calling." What you do should always surpass you. The passion, talents, and gifts that God has given to you are only important if it's meeting someone else's need. It results in fruitfulness in the world.

THE TIME IS NOW

Because of the numerous things that we can do in life, it's very easy to withhold from doing what we should be doing. We tend to put off our calling day after day. What is this called? Procrastination. Procrastination is the contender of purpose, manipulator of productivity, and thief of time. It invites in anxiety, pressure, and unworthiness. It feeds off doubt, fear, and hesitation. It's the leader of indecision. Its number one source is laziness. It settles in our choices and hinders our development. Its favorite day of the week is tomorrow. Its reputation is unfinished business. It loves the word "later." Its best friend is daydreaming. It's related to sleep. Its measurements of accomplishments are zero. It hates discipline and loves relaxation. It takes to the grave aspirations, dreams, goals, ideas, plans, thoughts, and visions. We hate it with our words but love it with our actions. And again, we wonder why we're often unfulfilled in life.

For years, I shied away from what God was calling me to do. Speaking, teaching, and writing were things that I felt that I wasn't good enough at, so I continuously put them off. God was patient with me, and I finally answered His call. There is always something beneficial on the other side of fear and procrastination.

When you decide to take that leap of faith and do what it is that you sense God is calling you to do, know that life will try you, your flesh will tease you, the enemy will tempt you, and God will test you. You will and must pay the price of saying yes to The Lord's will. I say these things not to deter you, but to urge you to press forward even when things get tough. God is stretching your faith, and that leads to perseverance.

The average American lives to be about 80 years of age and works roughly 30-40 years their life. The majority of them will work at a job that they don't love and will sleep roughly a third of their life, which is around 25 years. If we take the average 80-year-old American and subtract 30 years of them working a job that they dislike and subtract 25 years of them sleeping, the average American is only left with about 25 years of life. In those 25 years, you must eat, commute, bathe, use the bathroom, get dressed, spend time with family, enjoy hobbies, etc. Over a lifetime, all of these necessities mentioned will cut into those 25 years of life. That may take you down to 10-15 years or even less. And, this doesn't even include your childhood. So when do you ever have time to accomplish what God has called you to do?

It's imperative for you to discover your purpose so that you can avoid wasting time doing something that you were never intended to do. Everyone isn't an entrepreneur, but we all are created for specific reasons ordained by God. Life is too short to not do what we're called to do. Psalm 39:5 says, "You have made my life no longer than the width of my hand. My entire lifetime is just a moment to you; at best, each of us is but a breath." If you look at your hand, you can see that the width of it is shorter than the length of it. If the Bible had said that our life is like the length of our hand, that would have been profound, but to say that life is no longer than the width of our hand sends a much stronger message. Our time on this earth is fleeting. We must pursue God's call for our lives right now.

Our calling is hard to find because it's hidden in the God that most Singles don't want to seek. If you don't have a clue of what your calling may be, pursue your passion because they both are interconnected. Passion is typically the gateway to your calling. We all have something that God has put in us to accomplish. Over 150,000 people die every day worldwide. Tomorrow is not promised to anyone. We must focus on our purpose in this season of our lives. We would hate to look back decades from now and realize that we weren't doing what God called us to do when we had the opportunity to do it.

"Our calling is hard to find because it's hidden in the God that most Singles don't want to seek."

CAN'T BE MARRIAGE ILLITERATE

Let's start by freeing Singles from believing the myth that you need to be married to know what marriage is about. Matter of fact, Singles should obtain as much knowledge as we possibly can about marriage before becoming a spouse, especially if that is our desire. If I had a dime for each time that a married person said to me "you're not married, you wouldn't understand," I would be a very wealthy man. Okay, I'm exaggerating a bit, but you get what I'm saying. Granted, there are many instances that only a husband and wife can speak on due to their marital experiences. However, this does not limit those who are unmarried from understanding this love-keeping covenant at its original intent.

Also, let's clear the air on another common misconception. There are two types of people in this world: those who are married and those who are Single. There is no in between or exceptions. If you are in a monogamous relationship, you are Single. If you are engaged, you are Single. If you are divorced or widowed, you are Single. The only time that you are not Single is when you have made a covenant commitment with someone of the opposite sex through some type of ceremonial occasion under governmental law.

I think it's safe to say that most Singles desire marriage. The problem is that many of us don't know the very basics of marriage or how to be a spouse. The relationship between a husband and wife is what constitutes marriage and is the bedrock of social order. The definition of marriage has now been altered by man, but still holds true by God. Regardless of the Supreme Court's decision to yield to political correctness, marriage is still a beautiful and God-ordained gift. Timothy Keller, author and pastor, says, "The Bible begins with a wedding (of Adam and Eve) and ends in the book of Revelations with a wedding (of Christ and the church)." It's truly something meaningful and sacred to God. Singles who have a solid understanding of the fundamentals of marriage are more than likely better prepared for it. The four basic principles of marriage are procreation, regulation, sanctification, and illustration. In this chapter, we will discuss these central components to marriage along with some other truths, but first, I want to share with you the genesis of marriage.

GOD DESIGNED MARRIAGE

Our culture, particularly Singles, is failing to comprehend what marriage was intended to be because we live in a world that appeals to the selfishness of our flesh. Relationships become more about a personal benefit, and when the demand isn't met, we move on. Someone once told me that marriage is strictly for business purposes. Unfortunately, this is the pulse of our society. Marriage in many cases is perceived as a hindrance to one's freedom (hence, the ball and chain mentality). Spending the rest of our lives with one person under the approval of God has become an ancient practice to countless Singles. But even in this sin-filled and fallen world, marriage can still be successful in God's sight because God created it, and we know that whatever God has produced is intended for His glory.

Marriage was God's idea at the beginning of time. Let that sink in for a moment. God established marriage, and it could never be considered as a man-made invention. Although everything that God created was good, in Genesis 2:18 God stated: "It is not good for the man to be alone. I will make a helper suitable for him." This Scripture reveals the deciding factor to the first man and woman becoming husband and wife. Marriage was once perfect when initially created, and the central part of the sinless world, but Adam and Eve's disobedience tarnished its original state. However, the purpose of marriage was, and still, is to reflect the covenant Christ has with the church. As Pastor John Piper would say, "most foundationally, marriage is the doing of God, and ultimately, marriage is the display of God."

The spiritual bond between a husband and wife is the first established institution at the beginning of human history. It precedes all other institutions including business, church, and government. It even takes precedence over the family because without a husband and wife, children couldn't righteously exist. Genesis 2:24 is echoed and elaborated further by Matthew 19:5-6 as it states, "For this reason, a man will leave his father and mother and be united to his wife, and the two will become one flesh. So they are no longer two, but one flesh. Therefore, what God has joined together, let no one separate." There are a few important things to point out in these two verses.

> "The spiritual bond between a husband and wife is the first established institution at the beginning of human history."

Firstly, Eve was formed directly from the body of Adam, which alludes to her being one with her husband, closer than all other human relationships including parents to children. Secondly, because a marriage requires a man to be united with his wife, he must leave the household of his parents to form his own as the two become one flesh, operating literally as one, expressing this interconnecting bond between husband and wife. Lastly, the next verse clearly shows that God is the unifier of a husband and wife by the two joining as one flesh. No man should come between the seal of a covenant and divide what

God has commenced. These Scriptures unmistakably clarify God's high regard for marriage. And it all began with Adam and Eve, the first marriage originated by the Originator.

It was God's initiative and inspiration. No human mind could conjure up such an awesome design, and marriage could not exist without both male and female. A man gave life to a woman, and a woman gave life to the world. There is no inequality amongst the two, but this is an accurate representation of how much we truly need each other in the context of a God-ordained union.

> "A man gave life to a woman, and a woman gave life to the world. There is no inequality amongst the two, but this is an accurate representation of how much we truly need each other in the context of a God-ordained union."

Since God made marriage a key feature in His creation, we as Singles should reverence marital relationships with great significance for earthly and heavenly reasons. In fact, Hebrews 13:4 tells us "Marriage is to be held in honor among all." God is holy, so marriage is to be cherished as holy. God is love, so marriage is to be treasured as love. It's an extension of who He is. Despite the world turning love-keeping covenants into lust-fleeting contracts, we still must hold fast to what God intended. His blueprint for marriage is still the undeniable structure for the world. Societies' inventions for families are trendy, but God's plan for all generations still remains.

BE FRUITFUL AND MULTIPLY (PROCREATION)

To have the privilege of bringing a child into this world has to be one of the most rewarding experiences life has to offer following salvation and marriage. This really resonated with me when one of my closest friends had his first child, a son. Every time that I hold him, I think to myself, "I cannot wait to have a son or daughter." Honestly, if it is in the Lord's Will, I'll have multiple. Yes, I'll admit that I've caught a case of baby fever, and although I long for the opportunity to become a father, I understand that having children falls under a greater scheme of things. While enjoying, loving, nurturing, protecting, and teaching our offspring is imperative to the tall task of parenting, Singles must grasp a deeper concept of childbearing.

The first command ever mentioned was in Genesis 1:28 where God ordered Adam and Eve to "Be fruitful and multiply. Fill the earth and govern it." Yes, marriage is designed for husbands and wives to make babies, but having children isn't the sole purpose of procreation. The essential part of having children is to train up disciples to reflect the image of God in the world, and what better way to do so than by having children of your own that can be spiritually taught the Word of God on a daily basis. Proverbs 22:6 says, "Train up a child in the way he should go, even when he is old he will not depart from it." The Great Commission can be successful right at home, beginning with the new additions to the family.

Speaking of family, another part of that command is for us to "fill the earth and govern it." When we raise up children to be genuine followers of Christ, we pass down biblical principles through generations of families that raise other generations of families that expand the reach of God all over the world, which ultimately enlarges the Kingdom. Imagine you and your spouse birthing four children. You raise those four children to be God's representatives on the Earth, and when they grow up, they get married and individually have four children of their own and instill in them the godly instructions that you first taught them. Eventually, those sixteen grandchildren will grow up and have children of their own and raise up more kingdom kids who will do the same, and the process will continue to repeat itself. The purpose of childbearing becomes much more essential when we as Singles can embrace the opportunity for Christ's name to be glorified through the seeds placed in the wives of the family, while husbands, who are the priest of their homes, are to disciple them.

ADVANCE THE KINGDOM (REGULATION)

When God created the earth, everything that He established was made with perfection and deemed "very good." The only time God regarded something as not good was when He said, "It is not good for man to be alone." Let's ponder on this. If Adam were created perfectly, and knew God better than anyone else in human history and had a clear understanding of his purpose, it would seem that he had all that he needed, right? God, being all-knowing, knew that for His kingdom to be advanced that Adam would need a companion that could help him to build upon what He had already started. Eve was created to be a suitable match to Adam. This is an element of what a kingdom marriage signifies.

Singles who desire marriage must choose someone who will align with what God is calling them to do. This will be your one-flesh ministry. When the two join together in matrimony, they devote their lives to each other by committing their lives to the cause of Christ Jesus. This is the mindset that both should have. Singles, it should be a red flag if the person that you are interested in has no desire to see souls saved, people served, and God satisfied. Single men, how can you expect God to bring you a help-mate when you have nothing for her to help you with? Single women, how can you expect God to bring you to the one that He called you to help if you have a problem with being a helpmate?

There was an older married couple from my church that was such a beautiful example of being ministry focused and advancing the Kingdom. To-gether, they served faithfully as ushers for many years. They would drive from Akron to Cleveland every Sunday to contribute to the flow of our church service. Over the years, the husband battled with cancer, but even that didn't deter him from serving the Kingdom with his beautiful wife. There were days when I came to church, and the encouraging hugs that I received from them instantly lifted my spirit. They were the epitome of a married couple serving others through their loving acts and willing-ness to edify the body of Believers. Recently, the husband was called home to be with The Lord, but his wife has continued serving in her role by doing what she has been called to do. The caring and com-passionate spirits that this couple embodied are what we need in this world, and I pray that God grants us with spouses that have a heart to serve like them.

The service that Singles and our future spouses are involved in doesn't have to be an extravagant world missionary ministry. It can be as simple as ushering like the awesome married couple from my church. Maybe the platform is larger, and God wants to use you and your future spouse to speak to the nations. Whatever it is, understand the importance of having the heart to serve. It is our collective calling.

CONFORM TO THE CHARACTER OF CHRIST (SANCTIFICATION)

One thing that has been evident with my married friends is their undeniable maturity. The selflessness that they have come to embody is incredible to witness. As mentioned in the first chapter, our goal is to glorify our Heavenly Father by becoming more like Christ. God uses marriage to eradicate sin and cultivate holiness in one another. With someone who is always there to hold us accountable, challenge us, and expect us to grow, Christ's character will inevitably be more apparent in our lives as we yield to the leading of the Holy Spirit.

As two inherently sinful human beings learn how to become one flesh under the authority of God and conform to the character of Christ through marriage, they must consistently engage in the act of dying to their selfish ambitions and desires. There will be some emotional clashes and mental disputes that will require self-denial and self-sacrifice for the greater good of their marital bond. This will be required day after day, week after week, month after month, and year after year. "I" must turn into "we", and "me" must turn into "us". The giving of oneself is the very nature that Jesus symbolized when He laid down His life for us, His precious bride. When marriage is portrayed the way He envisioned, the gospel is on display.

A PHYSICAL REFLECTION (ILLUSTRATION)

Marriage is much more than displaying compatibility and more than just sharing a life with someone. Marriage is much more than building an empire and showing the world that we finally have our "happily ever after" union. These are all wonderful, but marriage ultimately is the depiction of Christ and the church. Many Singles don't even understand what this means. So, allow me to clarify.

Here is something that is unpopular and not well received by the world, and even by some Christians. A crystal clear correlation to the conformity of Christ in marriage is the husband's headship and the wife's submission. In modern times, men and women have their disagreements about authority and submission because it's been abused and taken out of context. Many men take being the head of his wife as a dictatorship, and many women view submission as a weakness. Both beliefs are wrong.

> "A crystal clear correlation to the conformity of Christ in marriage is the husband's headship and the wife's submission."

Ephesians 5:21 says, "Submit to one another out of reverence for Christ." For starters, spouses, in general, are to be submissive to each other. This is not something only wives are supposed to do; both spouses should be submitting to one another out of respect for Jesus. Single women who may be hesitant about marriage because of this matter shouldn't be concerned if both husband and wife honor the way God intended marriage to be. Ephesians 5:22-24 goes on to say, "Wives, submit yourselves to your own husbands as you do to the Lord. For the husband is the head of the wife as Christ is the head of the church, his body, of which he is the Savior. Now as the church submits to Christ, so also wives should submit to their husbands in everything." Single women, it's your duty to submit to your husbands as the head of your household. This is a sure way for you to display Christ's work in you, and as hard as this may seem to be, it's commanded of you and presents an opportunity for obedience.

I can hear all the Single men yelling out "yeah, tell em!" Slow your roll, fellas. Let's look at Ephesians 5:25 where it says, "Husbands, love your wives, just as Christ loved the church and gave himself up for her." Single men, it's our duty to love our future wives with an undying and unwavering love as Christ loved the church and also sacrifice ourselves for her well-being.

Both spouses have a particular calling. Wives are called to submit to their husbands as they do to Christ. Husbands are called to love their wives as Christ loves us. Men aren't called to be rulers in a harsh way, and women aren't called to be followers in a weak way. If both callings are honored as biblical truths, husbands and wives will embrace their roles, and there would be far fewer issues about leadership and submission. It is necessary to comprehend this as a part of displaying the character of Christ. Most Singles enter into a covenant with their spouse without being aware that marriage should reflect an understanding of God's love and sovereignty.

SINGLES NEED TO KNOW THIS

If only one marriage is ending in divorce each year, that is one too many. No one who joins together in matrimony should be filing papers to permanently separate from one another regardless if it's in months, years, or decades. When a marriage is ripped apart, everything associated with it is negatively impacted. I've witnessed some married couples that I have admired get divorced, and to be honest, it's been very discouraging for me. I'm sure that it has been disheartening for you, too, if you have witnessed the divorce of any of your loved ones as well. But, why is this so prevalent? It's not just something that is occurring in the world; it's happening in the church also. Each scenario is different of course, but I believe that the underlying issue is shared in the book of Genesis.

When it comes to headship and submission, the answer sits in Genesis 3:16, shortly after Adam and Eve committed the first sin. God cursed both of them. This is what He said to Eve, "You will desire to control your husband, but he will rule over you." This is significant in understanding why husbands and wives are always at battle with each other. Initially, the marriage between Adam and Eve was in perfect harmony until sin entered the world. Because of Adam and Eve's disobedience, women were cursed with the sinful desire to challenge their husband's leadership by naturally struggling to submit, and men were cursed with the struggle to innately rule over their wives in a harsh and unloving way. This is why we see so many husbands leading their wives with an overbearing spirit, and wives lacking a submissive spirit. The beauty of salvation is that it frees us from the curse of harshly leading and grudgingly submitting, and allows spouses to joyfully operate in their respective roles through regenerating work of the Holy Spirit. We become empowered to love and submit to our spouses in the way Paul speaks about in Ephesians 5. This biblical truth should help Singles become more understanding before marriage. If we as Singles can empathize with the sinful struggles men and women both face, I believe that more Singles will have a better chance at marriage from the beginning.

WHAT'S LOVE GOT TO DO WITH IT?

Dietrich Bonhoeffer, a German pastor, once said, "It is not your love that sustains the marriage, but from now on, the marriage sustains your love." One of marriage's purposes is to enlarge us and make us more fruitful. Marriage exceeds far beyond the love that a man and a woman have for one another, and what it symbolizes is infinitely profound. In Gary Chapman's book, "Things I Wished I'd Known Before We Got Married," he said, "What is ironic is that we recognize the need for education in all other pursuits of life and fail to recognize that need when it comes to marriage." In the height of entertainment, along with social media, love has been advertised as a euphoric and romantic emotion that only people "in love" can feel. Our society has an intense craving for love, and whenever we see anything that resembles it flashed before our eyes, we believe that it must be love. We are constantly bombarded with love stories and happy endings, and it can begin to shift our perspective as if that is what we should be expecting. Now, I'm not saying we should not hope for love in a delightful way. I'm just noting that the love we often see isn't the love we should put our confidence in.

We as Singles are looking from the outside in and are tempted with believing that a husband and wife's love for one another is the sustaining factor of their marriage. This is marriage illiteracy at its finest and Singles must deviate from this idea. Our minds have been accustomed to believe that love is all about emotions and feelings, physical desires, and sexual affection. Yes, I agree that our spouse should make us happy, but we put so much emphasis on the good side of marriage that millions of people are setting themselves up for separation or divorce. How many times have we heard someone say that they don't love their spouse anymore or that they've grown apart, or fell out of love? These statements represent a conditional love. Marrying a spouse is not just about what we can get and the feelings they can give, but more about what we can give and how we can each grow.

Love is selfless and looks to serve. Even more, love is at its best when it is least reciprocated. It's easy to love someone when things are going well, but what about when they're not? Do not marry someone who desires you to meet every last one of his or her demands. That is not love. Paul Washer said it best, "How can you learn unconditional love if you're married to someone who meets all your conditions?" Love is more than an emotion; it is a decision to commit to loving someone unconditionally. That is Christ-like love that isn't well received by the majority because it commands us to love even when those honeymoon feelings are gone. Love demands more than words or thoughts, but actions and deeds.

> ## "Love is at its best when love is least reciprocated."

The ultimate sign of love in a marriage is putting God before our spouse, and putting our spouse before everyone else. Is that a decision that we can honestly make? Gary Thomas, the author of The Sacred Search, asked two profound questions: "Ten years after you're married, what kind of tears will you be crying? Will they be the stinging tears of pain or warm tears generated by joy?" I think you know what the answer should be.

So again, what does love have to do with it? It has everything to do with marriage, and if you can allow this meaning of love to be branded on your heart, you will be more equipped and prepared.

MISTER OR MISSES RIGHT NOW

It breaks my heart when I hear about a divorce. When a husband and wife split, I always wonder what their lives were like as Singles. There are tons of reasons for divorce, but the same ones seem to remain at the top of the list such as abuse, communication, finances, and infidelity. I understand that life happens and people have moral failures, but if we as Singles are more purposeful about our preparation, I truly believe there will be fewer divorces.

Know your worth. Heal from your past. Wait on God. Be content. Stay pure. Remain focused. Discover your purpose. Understand marriage. These are all fundamentals for Singlehood. This chapter will introduce and unpack two components that are pertinent to Singles, which are service and stewardship.

As Single men and women, getting into the act of serving is not only beneficial for us and our walk with God, but it trains our hearts for the acts of service that we will be providing to our future spouses. If we get into the habit of serving others, how can we not want to serve the one that we love? Also, managing our lives by becoming stewards over all that God has given us proves that we can be trusted by Him, but also prepares us to be responsible spouses when that time comes. Taking care of our business in the

Single season will surely help us to take care of our business in the married season. Let's discuss further.

UNDIVIDED DEVOTION

To have an undivided devotion to The Lord is to be single-minded in your commitment to Him. It means that you possess a focus that's purposed for the advancement of the Kingdom of God. The obligations and responsibilities of a Single man or woman are not divided, and that's a blessing even if you may not concur. I have encountered many Singles who are so disappointed about not being married that they fail to realize they have the freedom to explore many opportunities that they may never have while married. Our liberty for service is a privilege, not a burden, and we should do all that we can, when we can, where we can, and while we can in this season of Singleness. Paul spoke about this important matter in one of his letters.

> "Our liberty for service is a privilege, not a burden, and we should do all we can, when we can, where we can, and while we can in this season of Singleness."

1 Corinthians 7:32-35 says, "I would like you to be free from concern. An unmarried man is concerned about the Lord's affairs--how he can please the Lord. But a married man is concerned about the affairs of this world--how he can please his wife-- and his interests are divided. An unmarried woman or virgin is concerned about the Lord's affairs: Her aim is to be devoted to the Lord in both body and spirit. But a married woman is concerned about the affairs of this world--how she can please her husband. I am saying this for your own good, not to restrict you, but that you may live in a right way in undivided devotion to the Lord."

In these verses, Paul is comparing the married and unmarried positions of serving. He starts off by saying that he would like for us to be free from the concerns of marriage because the unmarried have more opportunities to serve and please God with fewer distractions. Married people have to focus not only God's mission but also their spouses and families. This is a clear indication that we're to maximize our Singleness with service. Paul doesn't want to hinder us from marriage, but if we're not married yet, let's stop sitting around hoping for a spouse to complete us and go finish what God has called us to do in this season. Here is an example an opportunity that I was afforded in my Singleness.

> "Let's stop sitting around hoping for a spouse to complete us and go finish what God has called us to do in this season."

On December 14th of 2012, our nation was traumatized by the senseless act of violence that occurred at the Sandy Hook Elementary School in Newtown, Connecticut where innocent students and educators lost their lives at the hands of a gunman. Hearing the news of any senseless death can be heartbreaking, but to learn that many of the victims were children, who had so much life ahead of them, touches a special place in our hearts. Shortly after the news broke, a friend of mine called and stated that a church was taking a bus trip to Newtown to serve and support the residents, and asked if I wanted to join. Without any time to go home and prepare, I eagerly accepted.

Once we arrived, we met at the city's town hall to make signs, love on and pray for the victims' families, and mourn with those who were hurting. Later that evening, we attended a worship service at a local church. The entire sanctuary was filled to capacity. As we entered, they allowed us to stand along the wall. To further illustrate this picture, imagine roughly 20 black men and women walking into a predominately white church. You should have seen the heads turn. I must admit, it was a little uncomfortable at first. But in the middle of the pastor's message, he stopped and said, "I just got word that we have supporters here from Cleveland." Everyone in the sanctuary stood up and gave us an applause of appreciation. It was an incredible moment. After service, we had the opportunity to fellowship with members of the church. The love in that room was unbelievable, and I was beyond thankful that I could make the trip.

Looking back on this incredible experience, if I were married, I might not have been able to attend since it was such a last minute request. One of my closest friends, a newlywed at the time, was unable to go due to his marital responsibilities and not being able to leave his wife on short notice. As a Single man or woman, you have ample opportunities to serve and make a difference in your communities or the world. Capitalize on as many chances as you get. This doesn't mean that you'll never have opportunities for service once you are married, but instead that your first priority will always be your spouse and children. There will be times when the duties of a family will have to take precedence over any possible chance to assist in a cause or anything that you'd desire to do, even if it's for the glory of God.

Personally, I recommend that every Single have a period in their life where they abstain from dating relationships for at least six months to a year. Not only does this express a sign of faith, love, and sacrifice to Christ Jesus, but it also allows your relationship with Him to be strengthened. God is calling us to be in covenant with Him and the best way to do so is to give Him your complete devotion. No, this is not a command from God, just a suggestion that I believe is good for us. Let's look at five key areas of our lives that we can make better as Singles.

THE FIVE ESSENTIALS

When God first put the idea on my heart to write this book, these five important fundamentals instantly came to mind. The point of these essentials is to encourage those to redirect their focus on the importance of stewardship that leads to the path of intentional growth. The goal isn't perfection; it's preparation. I believe that an emphasis on these particular areas of life will not only help us to be better prepared as spouses but will also help us to be better individuals.

Spiritual Maturity

All throughout this book, I've placed heavy emphasis on our need for God, but being saved is only the beginning of our journey, not the end. Spiritual maturity is about becoming more like Christ through the sanctifying work of the Holy Spirit, which produces a life marked by obedience that is rooted in faith and love. This is vital to know because Jesus isn't just our Savior, He's also our Lord. Many Singles want the redemption of God, but not the rule of God. What I mean is that it's easy for us to live our lives knowing that He's Savior because it means He has saved us from eternal damnation. However, it's much harder to live our lives as if He is Lord because that means that we have to surrender every part of ourselves to Him, and this is a sign of spiritual maturity.

"Spiritual maturity is about becoming more like Christ through the sanctifying work of the Holy Spirit, which produces a life marked by obedience that is rooted in faith and love."

To grow spiritually, we have to first acknowledge that we can't grow by ourselves. John 15:5 says, "I am the vine; you are the branches. If you remain in me and I in you, you will bear much fruit; apart from me you can do nothing." We feed and strengthen our spirit man through godly disciplines such as Bible reading and studying, prayer, fellowship, service, and stewardship. Daily devotionals and the active membership to a local body church will be the facilitators of these disciplines. Nevertheless, being a follower of Christ isn't about a set of rules to maintain or a to-do list to check off. It's about having a close relationship with our Heavenly Father, and this makes all the difference.

Spiritual maturity is imperative for Singles because too many of us are eager to build a foundation with someone when our own foundation in Christ isn't secure. Single men who are developed spiritually are more equipped to lead, and Single women who are developed spiritually are more equipped to be led. Focusing on your vertical relationship will consequently bless your significant horizontal relationship. As we continue to press toward the mark of the high call in Christ, we will gradually see ourselves maturing in ways that we could never imagine.

Physical Wellbeing

Health wasn't something I took serious until a few years ago. Ignorantly, I thought that going to the doctor was for those who were ill or elderly. Having been afforded the opportunity to be employed by a world-renowned hospital changed my perspective. I was able to work closely with healthcare professionals on a daily basis, which gave me a different outlook on the physical welfare of others and myself. Physical wellbeing is preserving the external and internal aspects of the human body through lifestyle behavior choices, which ensures health.

> "Physical well-being is preserving the external and internal aspects of the human body through lifestyle behavior choices, which ensures health."

I'm far from being a health and wellness expert, but there are some core principles that I'm aware of when it comes to living a healthy life. Focusing on the wellbeing of our physical nature includes consistent exercise, proper dieting, and regular sleep. All three components discipline and train the body for our benefit. If working out for you is somewhat of a drag or you just have no desire at all, start with small goals. Don't overwhelm yourself with unrealistic plans. Go to the gym once or twice a week, and allow the momentum to build over time. If time is an issue, find creative ways to incorporate a workout that runs parallel with your lifestyle. Furthermore, make sure that you're eating properly, or exercising may defeat the purpose. I think we all know that McDonald's isn't a healthy choice for a meal. And lastly, make sure that you give yourself adequate time to sleep. There's nothing cool about bragging about how you're not getting any sleep because you're up all night "grinding." Get some rest so that your body can recuperate.

Also, just as nice as it is to be and look healthy on the outside, it is even more important to be and feel healthy on the inside. It's beyond imperative for us to establish a relationship with a Primary Care Physician (PCP) so that our health is tracked and understood by the doctor that we regularly visit. We as Singles must educate ourselves on choosing the right PCP suitable for us, and stay with that doctor unless there is a reason to transfer care such as location change, doctor retires, etc. Exercise, diet, and sleep represent preventative care, but establishing regular check-ups with a PCP is also preventative as well.

Preserving the quality of our lives can prevent sickness, improve moods, and boosts energy. Our bodies are the temple of the Holy Spirit given to us by God, and we should honor Him and ourselves by taking care of it the best way that we can. If you don't take care of your body, your ability and effectiveness for the Kingdom may decrease. It's impressive to see Single men and women who are serious about their inward and outward health. It represents commitment, discipline, and a passion for being our best self. This should be every Single's goal. It doesn't mean that we have to become fitness fanatics or look like magazine models, but we should show initiative for our physical condition. It's essential for either marriage or Singleness.

Emotional Stability

Life can be blissful today and stressful tomorrow. One minute you're up, the next minute you're down. It's obvious to see how the times of our lives can impact the way that we feel. When we're not steadfast in heart, our actions will reflect what's going on internally. When you don't express how you feel, you symbolize the unspoken. Emotional stability is the capacity to maintain balance and self-control of feelings during moments that threaten stable temperament. Allowing emotions to dictate our lives or denying our emotions all together are both unhelpful and ungodly. This is why self-control, a characteristic of the Fruit of the Spirit, is a must. Understand that the flesh should not control our emotions. The indwelling work of the Holy Spirit must assist our responses to our feelings.

> "Emotional stability is the capacity to maintain balance and self-control of feelings during moments that threaten stable temperament."

As you know, there are plenty of instances that make us want to react in ways that violate love. This is where the Holy Spirit plays His role as the one who convicts and corrects us for the sake of glorifying Christ whenever we want to react according to our flesh. You need God to manage your emotions, and that happens by getting closer to Him. Furthermore, controlling our emotions rather than allowing our emotions to control us is fundamental to the steadiness of our feelings. For instance, if you find yourself responding to a situation with irritation, it would be beneficial to stop, determine the reason for your anger, examine your heart to define why you're upset, and then respond in a way that's biblically rooted. Our participation in becoming emotionally stable is required, but please know that the steps that we take can never replace the work of the Holy Spirit. Submitting to the Holy Spirit is the way that we demonstrate healthy emotions that align with God's holy attributes.

Emotions that aren't under control are displeasing to God, wounding to others, and harmful to self. As a Single, it's important to develop emotional stability in this particular season of your life for the sake of your relationships and to become a better person. The quality of your relationships is often times a reflection of the quality of your emotions and how you manage them. Also, if you desire to be a spouse in the future, it's even more important to establish an emotive balance. No one wants to marry a Negative Nancy or a Petty Patrick, let alone be around one. Let's get those emotions in tact.

> **"The quality of your relationships is a reflection of the quality of your emotions."**

Mental Protection

God is the Creator of the human intellect, which provides us with the ability to analyze, organize, and rationalize. Even more, the mind has the capacity to learn, remember, understand and make everyday life decisions. It's one of our greatest assets. Although our mind is complex and sophisticated, it's still limited and in need of God's wisdom. Mental protection is the consistent guarding and renewing of the mind to maintain an eternal and godly perspective. Our minds are the battlefield in which the enemy attacks because this is where sin begins. We can easily be impacted by the enemy's deceit if we don't develop a mind for Christ. As we shield and feed our minds, we'll become more strengthened in mind.

First, we need to acknowledge that although our mind is beautiful and beneficial, it's also destructive and disastrous because it's infected by sin. Since we're naturally sinful even in our mentality, we have to continuously guard it. We are innately bent on believing deceits. Rather we conjure up our own incorrect thoughts, allow the enemy to deceive us, or believe what's going on in the world, we tend to trust the false testimony that is given to us by others or ourselves. This is dangerous because what we believe will shape our actions and display in our character. Proverbs 23:7 says, "For as he thinks within himself, so he is." In other words, keep in mind that you are what you keep in your mind. Instead of negative thoughts, we should focus on the continual reflection of godly things that help establish the right mindset. Philippians 4:6-8 says, "Do not be anxious about anything, but in every situation, by prayer and petition, with thanksgiving, present your requests to God. And the peace of God, which transcends all understanding, will guard your hearts and your minds in Christ Jesus. Finally, brothers and sisters, whatever is true, whatever is noble, whatever is right, whatever is pure, whatever is lovely, whatever is admirable--if anything is excellent or praiseworthy--think about such things." From these Scriptures, we can conclude that praying to God and refocusing our thoughts are two useful ways to guard our minds.

Also, when I think about guarding my mind, I reflect on who I surround myself with and what I allow to access to my mental. 1 Corinthians 15:33 says, "Bad company corrupts good character." If you're going to be serious about protecting your thoughts, you can't be around people who are carnal-minded and negative in their speech. It will only be draining for you, and eventually, you'll become carnal and negative-minded as well. Even more, you have to be careful of what has easy access to your mind. If you feed your mind garbage, your life will be a waste. Your thoughts manifest life; protect it from what influences it.

Second, we must remain in a constant state of learning. How do we do this? Read! Read! Read! We have to fall in love with gaining knowledge and applying wisdom. We have to renew our mind with Scripture. Guarding our thoughts is important, but it isn't enough. Imagine if you didn't feed your physical body with food for a few days. Without a steady diet, you'll eventually get weaker and weaker. This is no different with our spiritual mind. If we don't continue to replenish our mind with His Word, we won't be able to develop a mind rooted in Christ. Ephesians 4:23 says, "Instead, let the Spirit renew your thoughts and attitudes." When we refill on the Word of God, our minds will be transformed for the will of God, and when we know the will of God, we'll have a better outlook on eternity. Wise people seek knowledge.

> ## "If you feed your mind garbage, your life will be a waste."

It's important to develop the right mindset through guarding and renewing. Single men and women already have many pressures to deal with. Getting into the habit of pondering on godly thoughts and associating with people who'll be friends to our spiritual mind will mold and shape us into who we're called to be. If God sees fit, we'll be much better spouses with the proper mindset al-ready established beforehand. Although we'll always battle with our thoughts, these truths are essential to practice.

Financial Security

Finances are always at the top of the list of reasons for divorce. Each year, thousands of Singles commit to one another in marriage with little to no mutual understanding of how they'll manage their money. In most cases, it's because we're financially illiterate in our season of Singleness, and we lack the knowledge that we need to be prepared in this area. Although it's nice to be well off, being secure isn't about having a bunch of money in the bank. Financial security is having a peace of mind about the condition of one's economic situation. Solving money problems goes much deeper than what the common eye will ob-serve. It's a heart matter dealing with the mind, will, and emotions, but it can be less complicated than we make it.

"Financial security is having a peace of mind about the condition of one's economic situation."

If we're going to get a grip on our financial state, we must first choose God over money. Matthew 6:24 says, "No one can serve two masters. Either you will hate the one and love the other, or you will be devoted to the one and despise the other. You cannot serve both God and money." This is the first and most important thing we need to understand about finances. We honor God above all. Money can never be a priority over Him. Next, we have to stop saying, "money is the root of all evil." We're misquoting Scripture, and this sends a message that money in itself is bad. 1 Timothy 6:10 says, "For the love of money is the root of all kinds of evil." Loving money is what causes us to be pierced with many sorrows because it can very quickly become an idol in our lives that leads to sin. Lastly, we need to have a sense of balance with our finances. Proverbs 30:9 says, "For if I grow rich, I may deny you and say, 'Who is the LORD?' And if I am too poor, I may steal and thus insult God's holy name." Being rich or poor can cause temptation in different ways. I'm not saying that we should avoid having money, but our heart must be in the right place whether we amass great wealth or not, or money can potentially ruin us. Keep these Scriptures in mind.

When you have a better understanding of money, you can take the practical steps towards financial security. Five simple steps to consider are to tithe, save income, eliminate debt, cover expenses, and increase income. Firstly, tithing isn't something that we do because we'll be cursed if we don't. We tithe out of faith and gratefulness to our God. We give to the church to advance the kingdom of God. Secondly, paying ourselves next is important. We have to treat our savings as an expense, not an option. Thirdly, the Bible tells us to owe no man anything except to love him. We should be fighting to lower our debt as much as we possibly can. Fourthly, staying on top of bills and paying them in a timely fashion is kingdom-like. We should also focus on living within our means. Lastly, growing our income is important. I say this not because money is the be-all-end-all, but because we know that it's imperative to take care of the necessities of life. Money is a resource to support others and ourselves.

> "Money is a resource to support others and ourselves."

If we can learn how to maintain and manage money from a biblical perspective, it will not only prepare us for our future spouses, but it will help us be the best stewards that we can be as Singles. Countless Singles are facing credit issues, debt issues, and money issues that all impact financial security. We don't want to go into a marriage with a poor financial mindset. I'm not saying that we have to be debt-free with an 800 credit score and lots of money in the bank before marriage, but we can move towards that direction right now. Wealth is a major factor in our lives, and we must take it seriously. As Lynn Richardson, author of Check To Monday says, "Wealth means wisdom, expansion, assets, love, theology and health because I believe that wealth is not just about how much money you have in your bank account, it's about establishing harmony in your personal life."

Overall, we're free in Christ. Our lives are based off a radical relationship, not religious rituals. We must maximize on all activities and live this life with great passion. Let's make the most of our time with God, our personal relationships, our ministries, our finances, our bodies, and our lives. Pursue dreams. Explore often. Learn abundantly. Serve faithfully. Create inspirationally. Grow undeniably. Give cheerfully. We must be all that God has called us to be in this season of our God-given lives. It will prepare us for the season to come, Lord willing.

INTENTIONAL DATING

Before I understood the proper way of dating, I did whatever I wanted to do. There were times when I dated multiple women simultaneously, and there were times when I dated exclusively. Regardless of my approach, I still had no clue as to what I was doing. I had a "go with the flow" or a "whatever happens, happens" mentality. If I were given some foundational tips, maybe connecting with someone would have been more meaningful to me. Instead of dating aimlessly, I would have engaged in intentional dating.

Remember that this is not a dating book; it is a preparation book. Although this chapter is about Singles engaging in potential dating relationships, it focuses more on the preparation and understanding of dating. This chapter is all about intentionality in dating. Many times we think that being intentional begins at the point of meeting someone, but it actually begins long before we start to date. Here are some essential questions that you should ask yourself before you decide to date:

- Do you know who you are in Christ?
- Have you understood the purpose of your existence?
- Are you healed from emotional wounds such as past relationships?

- Can you honestly say that you are content in Christ?

- Do the pressures from society keep you in a constant state of discontentment?

- Are you struggling with the temptations of lust?

- Do you know what God has called you to do in this season?

- Do you understand the basics of marriage?

- What actions have you taken in preparing yourself to be a spouse?

I believe these are some questions that every Single should address before attempting to be intentional with anyone. Remember, the goal is preparation, not perfection. So, what is the purpose of intentional dating? It is two Christians discerning one another's ability to achieve God's purpose for marriage. When two Singles intentionally date, they are attempting to learn more about each other's character before they make a decision to commit. Intentional dating should lead to a relationship, and that relationship should lead to marriage. When Singles intentionally date, they already understand that marriage is the ultimate purpose of dating. This process should be taken seriously, yet still be enjoyable. This doesn't mean we instantly aim for a covenant the moment we meet someone, but it does mean that we keep the purpose of dating in the forefront. Having a marriage mindset is a prerequisite for dating.

Marshall Segal, editor of Desiring God said, "While the great prize in marriage is Christ-centered intimacy, the great prize in dating is Christ-centered clarity." I couldn't have said it any better. The reason why I firmly believe in dating intentionally is that it leaves no room for ambiguity. Dating should not be confusing; it should be clarifying. A God-ordained marriage should be the primary goal when aiming for a relationship. God is intentional, and if we are not, our dating efforts will not succeed to His standard.

> ## "Dating should not be confusing; it should be clarifying."

THE NON-NEGOTIABLE OF DATING

With a clear-cut understanding of intentional dating, let's lay down some foundation so that an unshakeable truth that remains. The Bible is filled with much to say about how spouses are to live while married, but really nothing about how Singles are to be when dating. The reason being is because there is nothing in the Bible that mentions dating, as it only references engagements and marriages. The best counsel for Singles is found in 2 Corinthians 6:14 where it tells us to not be unequally yoked with unbelievers. Every Single has different deal-breakers when it comes to dating. For some, a deal breaker would be someone who already has children, while someone else may prefer someone who is already a parent. Some, but not all deal-breakers can be overlooked or worked out. However, the Bible explicitly tells us to not date outside of the Christian faith. This is non-negotiable when it comes to dating. Please understand that this is a command from our God, not a choice for our flesh. We cannot disobey just because we dislike God's order. We must establish upfront that as Singles who want to honor Christ that we will only date Believers. We must settle in our hearts that we will refuse to date anyone who does not share in the faith of Christ before we even consider dating.

The rebuttals that Singles have for this dating command are endless. Believe me, I have heard them all. Some feel that it decreases the dating field, while others argue that Christians can use dating a non-believer as an opportunity to save souls. I have even heard of newly saved Christians who were in relationships with non-believers before accepting Christ in their lives choosing to stay with their agnostic partners. Yes, all of these are logical responses, but they still do not uphold God's Word. Believing that the dating field is limited is false. All you need is one spouse, and according to His will, whomever God has for you will manifest. Additionally, believing that we can use dating as a tool for evangelism is not wise and sounds more like a compromise. In fact, trying to date and evangelize simultaneously can be distracting for the both of you. If you honestly care about their salvation, you will guide them to someone who can disciple them and if it is God's will, the two of you will reunite. Furthermore, believing that you can change someone that you are already committed to is probably the number one mistake that Singles make. The enemy loves to falsely empower and swiftly deceive us into thinking that we are the ones who can initiate someone else's growth. No one who is inherently sinful can change another individual who is inherently sinful. This requires the regenerating work of the Holy Spirit.

> "Believing that we can use dating as a tool for evangelism is not wise and sounds more like a compromise."

Try to envision two bulls that are joined together by a wooden bar, which is attached to a heavy load that they both must collectively pull to reach an endpoint. If the bulls are unequally yoked, that means that there is a difference in height and strength. They also may not agree on the location of the endpoint. Whatever the advantages and disadvantages are, the two bulls are on separate pages, and the bull that is taller and stronger has to shoulder the greater weight to the point of overwhelming exhaustion. Additionally, the two bulls are pulling against each other if they are going towards different destinations. It becomes nearly impossible for the you, the stronger bull to reach your destination because even with you working the hardest, you end up dragging the other bull. This is what it is like when we date unbelievers. Christ is our objective that we press on to. If we are dating someone who lacks the spiritual foundation of Jesus, they are like the short and weak bull that we drag along this journey, even when they are pulling against us. We become fatigued from battling with them instead of exerting all of our energy on the mission of reaching our destination.

Singles must understand that our primary reason for existence is because of God. If the person that you are dating does not facilitate in developing your relationship with God, then you must cut them loose. Someone who claims to be interested in you but does not have a heart after God is a major contradiction. You cannot have a God-centered dating relationship that is divided or lacking in faith. Amos 3:3 rhetorically ask, "Can two people walk together without agreeing on the direction?" Of course not. No matter how scarce the dating scene may seem, or how attractive, caring, or intelligent that person may be, or how much you want to see their salvation come to pass, if they are not Believers of Christ, please disengage yourself. There are not any other biblical guidelines to dating that leads to marriage, but there are principle-based Scriptures that speak of the wisdom that we need for the decision to date.

DATING TYPES AND OUTCOMES

There are two mindsets to dating: Singles who date casually and Singles who date exclusively. There are two outcomes to dating: Singles who do not marry and Singles who do marry. I've observed Singles who date casually or exclusively, yet with no intent to marry and I've also observed Singles who date casually or exclusively with the sole purpose of marriage. Dating exclusively with marriage as the end goal is the right approach, but before I share with you the true meaning of dating, let's discuss the different types of dating.

Casual dating with no purpose of marriage should never be an alternative for Singles who are attempting to date the way God intends. The reason being is that there is absolutely no purpose for two Singles engaging in a dating relationship if marriage is not the goal, and it always leads to giving into the temptations of our fleshly desires. This is the complete opposite to intentional dating. According to worldly standards, aimless and casual dating is the most popular way to date. Hooking up with multiple partners may seem harmless, but it will produce emotional discomfort and spiritual emptiness. Since casual dating is unintentional, there is not much focus on getting to know the other person, and that leads to a lack of care and understanding. With no real connection between the two, sexual pleasure typically becomes the focal point. With no aim, you are destined to travel anywhere fast or nowhere at all, and you have no way to measure the growth of the dating relationship. This is the worldly way of dating, and Singles who desire to honor God must stay away from this method of connecting with other Singles. We cannot treat dating as a mindless activity. It should always be a purposeful engagement.

Exclusive dating with no purpose of marriage may seem commendable from the outside looking in, but it is actually the most dangerous way to date. Singles who are interested in being in a relationship with someone but never see matrimony in their near future defeat the purpose of dating exclusively. Exclusive dating with no aim of marriage often results in couples cohabitating, which puts the couple in danger of falling into sexual temptation. Society has become more accepting of this, but most importantly, God is not pleased with this type of dating. Without marriage in mind, hearts get broken, relationships get destroyed, and time gets wasted. Say no to a long-term relationship and yes to a long-term marriage. Our aim is a covenant, not a contract.

Casual dating with the hopes of marriage aligns with what God intends because of the desire to marry, but it can still be displeasing if done the wrong way. Some Singles understand the importance of marriage, but still battle with dating casually and frequently. When Singles pursue marriage by hopping from one casual situation to another, it may speak to a level of desperation that stems from impatience and loneliness. Ultimately, this type of dating lacks faith because the focus is more on what we desire instead of what God desires for us, and we tend to go out of turn. This results in premature relationships that most likely do not end with marriage or if marriage does happen, it was more than likely forced or rushed. Forced or rushed relationships are situations that we must avoid. Being Single is not intended for testing the waters, it's intended for testing the faith. This style of dating has a kingdom approach but is still worldly.

Exclusive dating with the purpose of marriage is the pleasing and proper way Singles should date. This is the responsible way of engaging someone that you are attracted to, and it speaks to the level of maturity that a Single man or woman possesses. How would you feel if someone expressed interest in you only to find out that they were pursuing or being pursued by someone else? I'm sure that you wouldn't like that, and neither would I. As we take our time in the dating process, not being so eager to bounce from one person to the next demonstrates patience and trust in God. Allowing Him to order our steps and present us to our spouse is the only godly way of dating. Dating shouldn't be a place for trail and error, but clarity and purpose. You don't date aimlessly hoping it all will work out. You date with the intent of building.

WHEN IS THE RIGHT TIME TO DATE?

Song of Solomon 2:7 says, "Promise me, O women of Jerusalem, by the gazelles and wild deer, not to awaken love until the time is right." I'm sure that you have heard someone mention "the right time" before. I know, it can be annoying, but it isn't something that we should minimize. This has to be one of the most puzzling questions for Singles, and rightfully so. Singles usually ask when is the right time to marry, but that implies that Singles are already in a relationship. What about those of us who have not gotten that far yet? We either give it too much or not enough attention at all. The right time to date will vary for each Single and is unique to their situation because everyone has different cultural upbringings and life experiences that contribute to their preparedness. There isn't a blueprint on the right time. Some Singles are ready to date leading to marriage the moment that they are technically legal, and some Singles may never be prepared in their lifetime. If you want to know when it's the right time to date, assess your spiritual maturity and discern God's timing.

As stated earlier, it is imperative for us to only date within our faith, but establishing our non-negotiable is only the foundation to intentional dating. Evaluating our maturity and preparedness for a dating relationship leading to a covenantal union requires an open and honest assessment of ourselves. Are we dating because we feel called or is our flesh leading us? Have we truly embraced the concepts of commitment and love? How have we demonstrated being great stewards over what God has already given us? Do we merely identify as Christians or are we actually living as Christians? Asking these questions gives us a guide to determining where we are. Additionally, the five essentials in the previous chapter are an excellent way to measure growth.

In many instances, Singles who want to date or decide to date have it in their minds the type of man or woman that they desire. There is nothing wrong with having a vision of your desired spouse, but that tends to only speak to what we want in a husband or wife, and not what we strive to be as a husband or wife. When we focus on becoming the equivalent of our preferred spouse, we are displaying an approved level of maturity. God will not send someone our way if we are not prepared because the right time is partially determined by our growth. It's almost as if you become a spouse in training before you date.

A popular saying amongst Christian culture is "worth the wait," but I'd like to ask, "are you worth the date?" This does not mean you are not worthy of being with someone, but it does demand the readiness of being a spouse. Since dating should be intentional in leading to a relationship that results in a marriage, we as Singles must be preparing ourselves to be a spouse. Those of us who feel called to marriage must work to become husbands and wives long before the wedding ceremony. So again, yes, you are worth the wait, but I ask, are you worth the date? Also, our maturity level goes hand and hand with the timing of God. God will never lead us to a potential spouse without our preparation for it.

Furthermore, although Singles themselves contribute to the right time to date, God is ultimately in control. The right time revolves around our preparedness, but even more, God's timing, and we must discern this. Proverbs 19:21 says, "Many are the plans in a person's heart, but it is the LORD's purpose that prevails,". God's timeline supersedes our preparation, no matter what we do. We must continually keep our spiritual ear bent towards what God is leading us to do. Sometimes we think we are ready to date someone when God knows that we are nowhere near it. You will know God is calling you to date someone by the constant promptings of your heart and the peace that comes from the undeniable desire. You cannot peacefully occupy someone else's life if peace is absent from your own life. We tend to fool ourselves into thinking that we are ready by forcing ourselves to believe that God approves. Our preparedness plus His perfect timing is the necessary combination for intentional dating.

> "You cannot peacefully occupy someone else's life if peace is absent from your own life."

SOUL MATE OR SOLE MATE?

When I was younger, and even when I first started to follow Christ, I entertained the idea of a soul mate. Believing that there was someone particularly made for me was very intriguing, yet intimidating. I became overly infatuated with the idea of how she should be. The problem with this belief system is that it creates a picture-perfect mentality. This type of thinking forced me to chase a person that I believed was made only for me, but unfortunately, that person doesn't exist. As I've matured, I've realized what I entertained was untruthful and only enticing to my self-centeredness. It was more so about me having what I wanted to have instead of becoming who I needed to be.

The Bible never speaks about a soul mate. To think there is someone exclusively made for you would indicate that in order for you to find your perfect match, every one else had or has to choose correctly

100% of the time, all throughout human history. Also, what about people who have passed away or gotten divorced or never decided to marry? Therefore, the idea of only one man or one woman being made particularly for another man or another woman is unbiblical, especially in an imperfect world. This should free Singles of any heaviness. The quest of discovering one person out of billions of people is intense, and God would not place that type of burden on us to bear. You do not have to live with that kind of pressure anymore.

Often times Singles are in search for a "match made in heaven" because we are confused by the secular beliefs that we hear and images of fabricated love that we see. We are sold the idea that we must be struck by cupid with an overwhelming experience of emotion to know that we have found our soul mate. Singles have come to believe they must have this experience or else the person is not "the one".

On the contrary, sometimes "waiting on God" can also paralyze Singles from even showing interest in someone when they are prepared to date. Due to over-spiritualizing beliefs, many Singles are depending on a particular sign from heaven. They believe that if God does not show them on a billboard or in a magazine or in some unusual way, that He does not approve. With this type of excessively religious thinking, many Singles believe that God has prohibited them from dating when He is actually all the more pleased with those who freely pursue potential spouses when they are mature enough to date. Being too deep can cause us to miss out on someone that has been right in front of our faces all along.

So, if we eliminate the idea of a soul mate, how do we know if someone is the right one? If you ever want to know if they are the one for you, know first that they are one with Christ. As Singles, sometimes we get too involved before we have evaluated the individual that we are interested in.

> ## "If you ever want to know if they are the one for you, know first that they are one with Christ."

To be perfectly honest, when you are truly walking with Christ and the time is right, you can choose to date anyone that you're interested in as long as they are Believers and are of the opposite sex. Of course there are other deciding factors such as attraction, connection, and chemistry, but Christ is the core reason for two Singles connecting. As you intentionally date someone leading to an exclusive relationship resulting in a covenant marriage, the two of you will become one flesh as Mark 10:8 says. Becoming one happens when two marry, not beforehand.

Essentially, that person becomes your soul mate, or better yet, your sole mate.

A sole mate is an exclusive and lifetime companion that we'll be led to. This person is someone whose life is securely positioned around Christ. This special and unique individual is already in agreement of what a biblical spouse should be. Your sole mate isn't someone who's still trying to decide if they want to put their faith in Christ or not. Although they are not perfect, their focus is on the mission of faith. Make sure they understand the fundamentals of marriage; procreation, regulation, sanctification, and illustration. Whoever we choose in marriage will become our "soul mate," solely. If the dating relationship is surpassing your knowledge of their character and holiness, things are going too fast. But if there's an undeniable observance of faithfulness to God and a sincere desire to serve Him, then they very well may be the one that God is leading you to.

All in all, regardless if you desire to be married or remain unmarried, God bless your journey of Singleness.